Growth Limitation and Political Power

This study was completed in 1974. Since then, the economic and political developments after the fourth war in the Middle East, especially the consequences of the drastic increase in the price of oil, have added emphasis to many of the basic points presented in this book.

Growth Limitation and Political Power

Bruno Fritsch

Ballinger Publishing Company ● Cambridge, Mass.
A Subsidiary of J.B. Lippincott Company

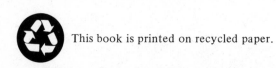 This book is printed on recycled paper.

International Standard Book Number: 0-88410-294-7

Library of Congress Catalog Card Number: 75-45497

Printed in the United States of America

Library of Congress Cataloging in Publication Data

Fritsch, Bruno.
    Growth limitation and political power.

    Translation of Wachstumsbegrenzung als Machtinstrument.
    Bibliography: p.
    Includes index.
    1. Economic   history—1945-   2. Economic   development.   3. World
politics—1965-   I. Title
HC59.F79313   330.9'04   75-45497
ISBN 0-88410-294-7

Dedicated to Karl W. Deutsch

Contents

Preface

Two basic events have changed the premises of future political actions on a worldwide scale:

• The transition from a world of abundance to a state of scarcity the June 1973 Strategic Arms Limitation pact between the U.S. and the U.S.S.R.

• The industrial nations are desperately attempting to minimize their dependence upon oil from the Middle East and other raw materials from the less developed countries.

A new globality is emerging: it is universal, intense, perfect and it expands swiftly. It comprises both technological and social phenomena; it is built upon the powers of acceleration, penetration and increasing complexity. Due to many accelerating factors within the sociopolitical realms, limits at least as real as those limits on economic growth dominating discussion today will occur at an earlier time than the exhaustion of natural resources. The true limits are within the realm of social and political adjustments. Therefore, the power issue comes in now—i.e., prior to the exhaustion of physical resources.

The actors participating in this power game are—besides the traditional nation states—the multinational corporations, the international governmental organizations and the international nongovernmental institutions. Altogether, some 10,000 "participants" with very different interests, powers, levels of information, etc. make the interaction of the total system increasingly complex. In this complex system, the structure of which is examined in the book, power operates. Because of their technological superiority, a core of industrial countries has the power to make much better use of the finite potential of the environment to absorb disturbances than the less developed countries have. This core group of highly developed industrial countries—about 15 altogether, "capitalistic" as well as "socialistic"—are in the position to achieve and to maintain a higher level of economic activity and yet have a lower environmental disturbance at the same time. Thus not only are they better off than the LDSs, but they can maintain their standard independent of the raw material resources of the LDSs.

The question then is how the international system can gradually shift from the present dominance-oriented structure to a more stable homeostaticly oriented, differentiated system in which dominance is replaced by participation, more equal distribution of power, justice and wealth. The required transition, being the only alternative to worldwide nuclear blackmail and war, has to be accomplished within a relatively short period of time. Therefore, the adjustment capability of the system must be improved by reaching learning institutions, by decentralization and by a rapid change of our values, norms and standards.

The critical paths in this process of transition are examined and the research—conducted on multilevel, hierarchial goal-seeking models—is assessed with respect to its validity as a means of solving these problems. Besides an extended bibliography, the book's appendix contains a number of tables related to these questions as well as a list of institutions and individuals dealing with these problems.

Acknowledgments

M. Burger and R. Frei were both invaluable to me during the preparation and analysis of the voluminous data. Sonja Meierhans contributed substantially to corrections; beyond this, she swiftly produced a reliable manuscript both in German and in English. Without the total cooperation of all involved it would never have been possible for me to complete this study on time. I would therefore like to express my gratitude to these people.

The text of this study was translated from German into English by Claire Reade. She had to deal not only with a complex subject but also with a relatively complicated German text. Due to her outstanding knowledge of the German language and to her understanding of the problems analyzed in this study, she managed both difficulties with admirable skill. I wish to express my sincere thanks for her outstanding work.

Zurich, March 1975   Bruno Fritsch

Growth Limitation and Political Power

Chapter One

The Situation in World Politics

FROM ABUNDANCE TO SCARCITY

The seventies have been distinguished, as Karl Deutsch appropriately remarked, by two basic events: first, by the transition from a world of abundance as prevailed in the Kennedy-Johnson era into a state of supposed scarcity, especially in the area of resources; and second, by the June 1973 Strategic Arms Limitation pact between the US and the USSR.* The visions of a "world of abundance for all" projected in the sixties—visions which seemed to reduce the contrast between private capitalist and state capitalistic economic order to a common denominator of increased consumer goods production—have disappeared. Today we are the witnesses of a fundamental consciousness change: the world has become finite for us; the boat is full; we have to accommodate ourselves to spaceship earth.

These two events have fundamentally changed the premises of political actions and will thereby deeply influence both the structure and the processes within the international system in the coming years. The battle over resources has already begun. The industrial nations are desperately attempting to minimize their dependence upon raw materials, particularly upon oil imports from the Middle East, while the developing countries sense a deadly threat to their existence both in the increasing environmental consciousness and in the emerging policies of growth limitation in the industrial nations.

While the agreement between the US and the USSR has brought no halt to the armaments race, it has nevertheless produced a mutual acknowledgement of the desire to avoid atomic war. The permissible

*The full text of this agreement is given in Appendix A.

level of conflict will thus shortly experience a substantial rise. Aside from this effect, the bilateral lineation of the spheres of influence gives each super power more scope for repression in the regions under its control. As early as 1968 the facts were clear: the United States would not interfere with the Soviet invasion of Czechoslovakia by using military force. Even clearer was the Soviet Union's self-restraint during and after the 1973 tragedy in Chile. Who can then be surprised that at practically the same time in both Czechoslovakia and Chile books were burned, and independent thinkers were being imprisoned or even shot? The same horrors occur at opposite ideological poles, but the details of the administration in whose name and under whose pretexts the suppression is perpetrated have very little effect on those afflicted or on the issues of freedom and human rights. The Soviet Union handles these matters with admirable consistency: it not only ruthlessly disposes of its own dissidents, especially those who do not yet have an international reputation; it goes one step further and vigorously denounces all leftist groups in the West who deviate from Moscow's party line, with exactly the same intention as the rightist advocates of "law and order." The official party terminology puts Anarchists, Maoists, Trotskiites and others in this category.[1]

There are essentially two main interests which unite the two superpowers in the current phase of world politics:

1. the aforementioned interest in avoiding all-out nuclear war and, deriving from that,
2. an inherent interest in surmounting growth limitations with the goal of further expansion of each country's productive powers.

The United States sends the Soviet Union grain and technical know-how, while the Soviet Union proffers gas and raw materials. This Ricardian trade should create a good relationship for the next ten to 15 years and foster an increase in export trade. In addition, the network of international investment, particularly between these two superpowers, will radically expand. Put in concrete terms, this entails construction of larger productive facilities with American capital and know-how in the Soviet Union, joint exploitation of Siberia's natural resources, expansion of scientific exchanges and closer cooperation in all areas of research, including space exploration.

All this should not obscure the fact that these two superpowers nevertheless pursue completely different societal goals and that, due to this fact, one can contemplate convergence of these two systems only in a very narrow sense. Although the United States and the Soviet Union are presently extremely interested in keeping Western Europe's political strength within bounds, the United States would also like to keep as many options open as possible for the further development of its relations with Japan, Mainland China, and with countries both within and outside the so-called "New Atlantic Charter." Underlining these problems is the great political weight attached to the growth limitations issue for the Western industrial nations. The question is whether the two superpowers, perhaps in conjunction with other industrial nations, could expand their growth potential with new methods of cooperation so that they become even less dependent upon the developing countries than they are now. The expansion of their own growth potential could proceed at the expense of and detriment to the future development possibilities of these less industrialized countries. Growth limitation is, therefore, a particularly important concept in power politics. It will mobilize very powerful political forces long before exhaustion of resources becomes an issue. It is this book's primary intention to investigate and examine the political problems and consequences of the international ecology crisis and to examine the validity of the thesis that maintains that the concept of growth limitation is nothing more than a new instrument for the domination of the haves over the have nots.[2]

THE NEW GLOBALISM

What is new about today's globality is its universality, its intensity, its perfection and the swiftness of its expansion. Today it encompasses both technological and social phenomena; it is built upon the powers of acceleration, penetration and increasing complexity. This globality is symbolized by the now familiar photograph of the earth taken from the moon by the astronauts in 1968. The contradiction between the states' claims of sovereignty and the global interdependence which is increasingly fostered by technology and its economic application stands in the center of this dynamic process. This increasing globality reveals itself most clearly in the problems of pollution and the exploitation of the world oceans. The conflict, now settled, between Iceland and Great Britain over the extension of territorial waters is only a modest precursor of much larger future conflicts. In addition to the fishing war between Iceland and Great Britain, the langoustino war between France and Brazil, and the crab war between Japan and the United States, other wars will undoubtedly erupt. The central conflict will not be over the extraction of foodstuffs but will be more concerned with the search for new raw materials—manganese, copper, nickel, cobalt, lead, iron and phosphate, not to mention oil. There are already charts in existence which project territorial limits into the high seas, so that nations on the opposite sides of the same ocean automatically become bordering countries. These charts would eliminate the difference between territorial waters and international sea routes. A completely new situation would arise, because regulation of the international shipping routes would require "transit corridors" through "national territory," a possibility which seems absurd to us today. In this connection, however, we must not forget that the mere extension of territorial waters from the classical three to 12 sea miles along with the consequences of "full national sovereignty" for over a hundred important seaways would seriously jeopardize unimpeded international maritime traffic. The upcoming sea rights conference, in which over 130 nations will take part, will have to deal with these and other problems.

It is not only the progress of scientific discovery which is accelerating; its economic applications follow within ever shorter time periods. Figure 1–1 clearly illustrates this phenomenon. One

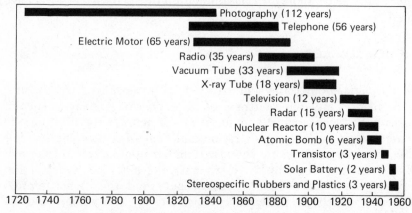

The acceleration of social change. This graph shows the increasing speed with which a technological innovation moves from discovery to practical application.

Adapted by the National Goals Research Staff from *World Facts and Trends*, published by the Center for Integrative Studies, School of Advanced Technology, State University of New York, Binghamton, New York, 1969.

Source: The Futurist Vol IV, 4 (August 1970).

Figure 1–1.

hundred and twelve years elapsed between the invention of photography and its application. With the telephone, it was only 56 years; with the electric motor, 65 years; with the radio, 35. Ten years elapsed between the construction of the first atomic reactor and its practical application; just a few years separate most pioneering inventions of the present from their practical—i.e., economic—application.

Technical advancement and economic growth interact reciprocally to release forces producing new acceleration and new global interdependence. A few examples will illustrate the point: developmental researchers concur unanimously that our know-how doubles every 12 years. This fact corresponds to a yearly growth rate of nearly 6 percent. The total volume of original scientific articles and annotations in 13 magazines of the American Institute of Physics has quintupled in 16 years.[3] This corresponds to a yearly growth rate of 11.24 percent. Technically utilized horsepower in the United States in 1948 totaled 2.8 billion; in 1967 it had already reached 17 billion, which corresponds to a yearly growth rate of 6.9 percent. Airplanes' top speed increased approximately 20-fold in 50 years; their transport capacity increased 40-fold in 30 years, while mobility, measured in billions of miles, has more than quintupled in the United States since 1940, implying a yearly growth rate of 4.9 percent. Direct American investment abroad almost tripled in eight years, and the tourist industry, as we all know, grows at a rate of between 7 and 15 percent per year. The negative consequences of this rapid change, however, are also increasing at a disquieting rate. Incidences of crime in the United States rose from 1.3 million to six million in the time from 1955–1971; that corresponds to a yearly growth rate of almost 10 percent. International telegraph traffic in the United States increased only slightly during the last ten years, due to the growing importance of the telephone. Consequently, the number of telephones in use rose from 66.6 million in 1958 to 115.2 million in 1969. One could continue with such examples forever; Table 1–1 cites a few cases, including the time these processes take to double.

The enormous rates of growth, higher than the gross national product of most countries for almost every example cited, are not the only noteworthy aspect of these statistics. The fact that the short doubling time must inevitably lead to critical situations is of vital interest. If, for example, crime in the United States were to continue to rise at the same rate, there would theoretically be a purely criminal population within 38 years, a patently absurd situation. The crime rate will therefore have to stabilize at some level in a population remaining roughly constant. That will be guaranteed not only through a stricter interpretation and implementation of the

Table 1-1.

Facts	Changes	Growth rate in % per year	Time of duplication (years)	Source
Total volume of scientific articles and annotations in 13 journals of the American Institute of Physics	1950: 1 million words 1966: 5.5 million words	11.24	6.51	A Buchholz, op. cit.
Increase of technically used horse-power in the US	1940: 2.8 billion h.p. 1967: 17.0 billion h.p.	6.91	10.37	John Waring, "The Horse-power Explosion," *The Futur-ist*, Vol. III, 1, (February 1969): 23.
Increase of maximum speed of combat planes	1925: 100 km/h 1970: 2,000 km/h	6.17	11.58	J. de Martino, "The Autonomy of Technology," *The Futurist*, Vol. II, 5 (October 1968): 93.
Increase of transport performance of military aircrafts	1940: 1,500 t/m/h 1970: 60,000 t/m/h	13.08	5.64	Ibid., p. 94.
Increase of mobility in the US (million passenger miles)	1940: 264 1975: 1,400	4.88	14.55	*A Proposed Program for Roads and Parkways* (Washington, D.C.: US Dept. of Commerce, Government Printing Office).
US direct investment abroad (in billion US$)	1950: 11.8 1970: 78.1	9.91	7.34	B. Fritsch, *Die Vierte Welt*, dtv, no. 929, p. 36
Increase of indictable offenses in the US	1955: 1,333,500 1971: 5,995,200	9.85	7.38	Federal Bureau of Investigation
Number of cables sent abroad (USA in thousands)	1963: 9,199 1970: 9,833	0.96	72.55	*UN Statistical Yearbook*, 1972
Telephones installed (USA)	1958: 66.63 million 1969: 115.222 million	5.11	11.60	Ibid.

Mail traffic: number of letters sent to and received from abroad (in billions, USA)	1958: 1,392 1970: 2,365	4.51	15.71	Ibid.
Foreign indebtness of less developed countries (in billions $)	1965: 37.466 1971: 79,218	13.29	5.55	World Bank Annual Report, 1973
Increase of UN member states	1945: 51 1973: 135	3.54	19.92	B. Fritsch, Die Vierte Welt, dtr, no. 929 p. 16, and The Stateman's Yearbook, 1973–74
Increase of foreign subsidiaries of multinational corporations (MNC)	1925: 800 1970: 7,267	5.03	14.12	Yearbook of International Organizations, 1st, 6th, 11th, and 13th edition, Union of Intern. Associations, Brussels (13th ed. 1970-71)
Increase of international non-governmental organizations (INGO)	1956/57: 985 1970/71: 2,296	6.23	11.47	Ibid.
Increase of international governmental organizations (IGO) e.g. UN organizations and european community	1956/57: 132 1970/71: 242	4.42	16.03	Ibid.
Defense expenditures (in billion $)	1949: 49 1972: 200	6.31	11.33	I. Kende, Local Wars in Asia, Africa and Latin America 1945–1969, Budapest, 1972, and SIPRI Report, Stockholm 1973

penal laws but also through a redefinition of what qualifies as criminal in a punitive sense. There exist, therefore, limits which cannot be overstepped within our system, not only in the realm of physical resources, but also, much more importantly, in the societal-technical realm. If we have a growth rate in air traffic today of 12, 15 and 17 percent, if the total foreign indebtedness of the developing countries grows at a yearly 13.3 percent, and if the volume of communications transmitted—for example, by telephone, postal system or the mass media—likewise expands, then signs of saturation will inevitably appear at some point. The entire world population cannot constantly be traveling or be solely engaged in receiving or transmitting news; nor is it more likely that the number of international organizations or multinational firms will increase at the same tempo, since every human would then shortly be employed by either one or the other. All of this reasoning, absurd as it seems, points in one direction. It indicates that limits exist in societal realms, limits at least as real as those limits on economic growth continually dominating discussion today—those imposed by the feared exhaustion of natural resources. We can even go another step and maintain that we will reach the limits in the realms of communication, information processing and the universality of our global relations earlier than in the realm of the economic-technical use of resources. It follows, then, that one must not examine technical-economic growth limitation isolated from these societal-political saturation problems. Figure 1–2 outlines this situation.

One can imagine the total problem in simplified form as a relationship of four subsystems. Subsystem I encompasses the human being and the population as a whole, as well as the problems related to the population explosion and the increases in aggression and conflict. All of these phenomena increase exponentially in time; they therefore grow at a constant *relative* rate. This is illustrated by the rising curve. Man's organization of society produces different societal systems: national states or the various forms of international nonstate organizations—multinational organizations, for example—all of which are included in subsystem II, a continually increasing function. Technology and its economic application represent the third exponentially increasing subsystem. Here the expenditures for research and development, as well as the numerous technical discoveries and innovations, are particularly important. Finally, subsystem IV, the natural environment, must be included in the overall system as the basis for all these processes. Both the resources, as well as the environment's absorptive capacity, are, like the environment itself, finite by nature. In contrast to the three

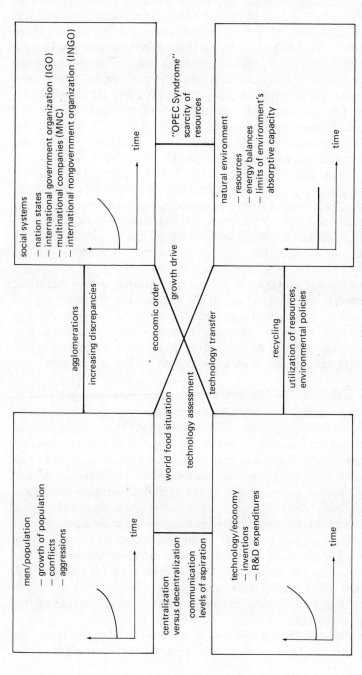

Figure 1-2.

previously mentioned subsystems, whose processes accelerate with time, the amount of available raw materials and, more importantly, the environment's capacity to absorb wastes are both finite and more or less constant. The relationship of these four systems produces a number of problems, due in particular to the inconsistencies between the three expanding systems and the fourth, both finite and constant. The relationship between subsystems I and II, for example, embodies the problems of agglomeration and increasing discrepancies in levels of economic and technical activity. Secondly, there is the problem of centralization versus decentralization, as well as the problems of communication and of levels of aspiration in connection with subsystems II and I, to which we will return later. The problems of the use of resources and of the environment's absorbtive capacity, including recycling, results from the relationship between subsystems III and IV. Finally, the connection between subsystems I and IV produces the political problem of scarcity of raw materials and the vital question of the political repercussions of this scarcity (OPEC syndrome).

There also exist a number of cross connections, as, for example, the one between subsystems I and IV concerning the world food situation. Let us examine, however, the connection between subsystems II and III. Here we meet the problem of technology transfer and assessment as well as the question of optimal economic order, not least important in its connection with the inherent drive for growth.

There are naturally innumerable other problems which have not been explicitly represented in this schema; the huge problem area of war, disarmament negotiations and the armament races, for example, is concealed behind "conflicts and agressions." The diagram merely indicates that one cannot only examine growth limitation in the economic realm; one must see the issue in relation to the technical, societal and, above all, political forces which determine economic growth.

If we examine the new globality, on the one hand, as a function of the degree of penetration as well as of expansion and universality and, on the other hand, in connection with the meaning which it has for both the future of the international system and for our survival, we can locate these problem areas within this network of inter-relationships. Figure 1-3 sets forth one possible presentation of this conceptual framework.

Such a representation is subject to a variety of opinion on the question of the location of the problem area. However, there is no

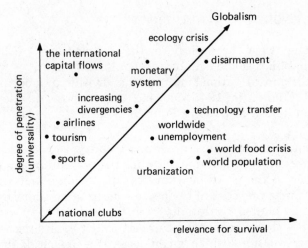

Figure 1-3.

doubt that although categories like airways, tourist trade and international athletics may reveal a high degree of penetration and therefore interdependence, they do not signify very much for our survival. On the other hand, the processes of urbanization and unemployment, as well as the population explosion and food scarcity, are highly significant for humanity's survival. Ecological problems as well as problems of arms limitation are decisive both on a universal plane and for future living conditions. In comparison, national clubs, to name only one counterexample, are in no way significant universally either for the future of the international system or for survival.

Let us summarize: The technical-economic processes of expansion are not just straining the limits of the physical sphere; limits will be reached beforehand in other highly varied realms which will result in a fundamental change of structure in our societal and international system and which will determine, definitively, the impact of the economic growth limitation upon the individual nations. The conflicts which will inevitably result from this transformation will probably be staged on a higher activity level, due to the American-Soviet detente.[4] The two superpowers' system of dominance will thereby conflict with the more ecologically oriented emancipation movements of today's developing countries.

COOPERATIVE OR COMPETITIVE GROWTH?

If everything went according to the conceptions of harmony developed in political and economic schools of thought, we would be sure of peace and of optimal international division of labor. Article I of the UN Charter in 1945 declared the purpose of the United Nations in imitation of Wilson's Fourteen Points of January 1918:

"1. To maintain international peace and security, and to that end: to take effective collective measures for the prevention and removal of threats to the peace, and for the suppression of acts of aggression or other breaches of the peace, and to bring about by peaceful means, and in conformity with the principles of justice and international law, adjustment or settlement of international disputes or situations which might lead to a breach of the peace;

2. To develop friendly relations among nations based on respect for the principle of equal rights and self-determination of peoples, and to take other appropriate measures to strengthen universal peace;

3. To achieve international cooperation in solving international problems of an economic, social, cultural, or humanitarian character, and in promoting and encouraging respect for human rights and for fundamental freedoms for all without distinction as to race, sex language, or religion; and

4. To be a center for harmonizing the actions of nations in the attainment of these common ends."

Article 2 of the UN Charter then describes the ground rules which should apply in the pursuance of these general goals. The end of this article states emphatically, however, that "nothing contained in the present Charter shall authorize the United Nations to intervene in matters which are essentially within the domestic jurisdiction of any state. . . ." This statement nullifies practically everything. The developments in world history since 1945 provide a rather clear and somewhat shocking balance sheet. From 1945 to 1970 there were more than 90 international armed conflicts. Not one of these wars was officially declared as such. The number of intranational conflicts and civil war altercations mounts into the thousands. Defense expenditures today amount to a round $200 billion dollars. In 20 years they have quadrupled; in spite of this increase, the relative share of defense in the gross national product has declined slowly since 1952. As we will later see, more than 80 percent of the total world defense outlay falls on the six most important countries—

namely, the USA, the USSR, Red China, France, West Germany and Great Britain. The developing countries' amounts to 10 percent.

The political conception of harmony stands as a counterpart to the economic one, which states in the theory of comparative cost advantages that every nation, for its own benefit, should devote itself to the production of those goods which it can produce at the lowest relative cost in relation to other competing nations. If this ground rule were generally adhered to, the theory claims, the economic development of each state within the realm of an optimal international division of labor would be guaranteed. Today we know, for many reasons which we cannot examine in detail, that this theory does not apply. We therefore have to recognize an increasing potential for conflict in the area of international economy as a counterpart to military development:

1. *The inequalities in income and property distribution* are increasing both within and between the individual nations. In 1971 the World Bank published the first comprehensive study, including data on the income distribution in a total of 44 developing countries. This shows, for example, that in Brazil 5 percent of the population receives 38.4 percent of the national income; in Gabon it is 47 percent, in Rhodesia 40 percent, in South Africa 39 percent, and so on. The complete table is printed in Appendix B.

All indexes suggest that these inequalities are not being reduced; on the contrary, they are even intensifying in certain countries. This situation raises weighty problems: by and large, the faster the growth, the greater the inequality in income distribution, because the higher incomes in general rise faster than the lower incomes during the process of economic growth. John Adler, director of the planning and budget division of the World Bank stated this dilemma in the following manner: "For example, is it 'better,' in some objective way, to have a period of sustained economic growth during which per capita *national* income grows at 3 per cent, and per capita income of the lower income groups at 4 per cent, or a growth pattern of which the national average rate of growth is 7 per cent, but the average of the lower income groups only 5 per cent?"[5]

2. *Worldwide unemployment* is increasing both absolutely and relatively. The number of unemployed in the industrial nations alone, a fact frequently overlooked, amounts to almost nine million people. In Latin America the figures rose from 2.9 million in 1950 to 8.8 million in 1965, and they are still rising. In India the population increases annually by 14 million; additional job opportunities should be created for about half of them each year but this has thus far

proved to be impossible. The unemployment rate for Pakistan, Sri Lanka, Malaysia and the Phillippines is estimated at more than 15 percent of the potential work force. Exact numbers are difficult to obtain, and comparisons with our labor market are practically impossible. It is still clear, though, that the number of people in the developing countries looking for work increases more quickly than in the industrial nations.

3. The number of people who cannot read and write is increasing absolutely, while decreasing relatively. One estimate states that the *world illiteracy quota* has sunk from about 43 percent in 1960 to 39 percent in 1965. Due to population growth, however, the absolute number of illiterates is higher today than it was 20 years ago.

4. *Agglomerations* (human clusterings) are increasing more rapidly than the population, particularly in the developing countries. The city population in the developing countries is presently estimated at 600 million. In the coming 30 years this will rise to three billion—an increase of 500 percent! The populations of the large cities in Latin America double every 14 years. Urbanization in developing countries is increasing rapidly. It thus produces problems which would be difficult to handle even with the highly technical and scientific expertise of today's industrial nations, not to mention with the meager resources available to the developing countries. Most of these countries find themselves in a per capita income bracket of between $100 and $400. As Figure 1-4 illustrates, the urbanization is increasing particularly sharply in this category. It is estimated that in 1990 more than 80 percent of the world population will be living in agglomerations—agglomerations which clearly do not deserve the label "city."

5. *The development gaps*—trade and income gaps—between the developing and industrial nations are still widening. This is a result of, among other factors, different growth rates and growth levels. It has been calculated that by 1980 the developing countries will show a trade deficit compared with the industrial nations of from $23–27 billion.[6]

One must not, however, merely reduce the differences between the developing nations and the industrial nations to the trade gap; Lester R. Brown strikingly summarizes this state of affairs: "The world is, economically speaking, two worlds—one rich, one poor; one literate, one illiterate; one industrial and urban, one agrarian and rural; one overfed and overweight, one hungry and malnourished; one affluent and consumption-oriented, one poverty-stricken and survival oriented."[7]

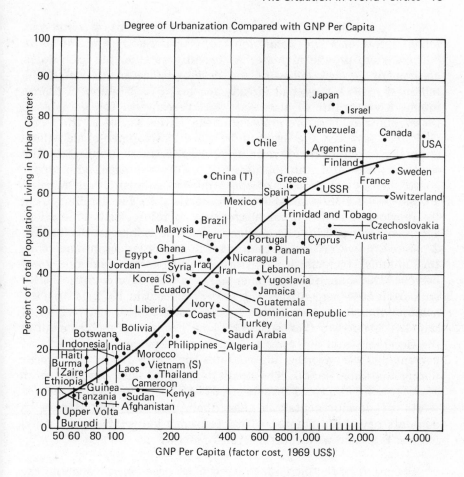

Degree of Urbanization Compared with GNP Per Capita

Reproduced from: "Urbanization," Sector Working Paper (Washington, D.C.: World Bank, June 1972).

Sources:

1. GNP per capita—World Bank Atlas, 1971.
2. Urban Area Population—Kingsley Davis. World Urbanization 1950–1970, Vol. I, University of California, Berkeley, 1969. Definition of "urban" is based on differing national standards.
3. Percent of population in communities of more than 100,000 for Table 1 in main text are from UN Demographic Yearbook: 1970, New York, 1971, Table 9.
4. Figures based on most recent census or estimated from sample surveys ranging from 1960 to 1970.

(1)Curve fitted to type $y = \dfrac{a}{1 + be^{-c(\log \text{GNP})}}$

Figure 1–4.

6. As a result of this very unequal development, *international indebtedness and the total debts of the developing countries in particular* are on the increase. As recently as 1965 the total dollar amount of foreign debts of the developing countries was $37.5 billion; by 1971 they had already reached $79.2 billion. This rise implies a yearly rate of increase of 13.3 percent; the foreign debts in these countries therefore grow more than twice as fast as the world GNP. The fact that the terms under which developmental aid will be given have deteriorated over the years further complicates the situation. The total contributions of the DAC countries, who supply approximately 95 percent of the total developmental aid, reached around $19.4 billion in 1972, in comparison to $18.1 billion from the previous year. The nominal sum rose, therefore, $1.3 billion—i.e., 7 percent. Considering the change in parity, this increase declined to 2 percent, however. If one then takes the rise in prices into account, this nominal increase is transformed into a *real reduction of 3 percent.* The share of developmental aid in the donor countries' GNP sank from 0.84 percent in 1971 to 0.77 percent in 1972, leaving the amount, therefore, even farther from the desired goal of 1 percent of the GNP. Added to that is the problem that the "grant" element in the developmental aid program slid from 57 percent in 1965 to 54 percent in 1971; average interest rates rose from 4.1 to 5.1 percent during the same period. The credit terms were also curtailed from 18.9 years in 1965 to 17.6 years in 1971.[8] This proves that the real worth of developmental aid has diminished and that decreasing amounts have been granted at less favorable terms—that is, at rising interest rates and with shorter terms of credit.

As a result of the increasing divergencies occurring throughout the world at an accelerating tempo, the development of world trade has shifted more and more to the already evolved industrial nations. The universality of world trade no longer exists. This fact is demonstrated on one hand by the collapse of the international monetary system and on the other by further limitations on the once universally valid most favored nation policy within the GATT. The UNCTAD has proposed a preference system for the benefit of the developing countries, instead of the symmetrical most favored nation role. The growth of world trade has suffered severely under these influences since 1968, going from around 12.5 percent in 1968 to less than 6 percent in 1970. The world trade has shown a rising growth rate only from 1971-1972 on. For 1973, the growth rate is estimated at a little more than 11 percent.

A very strange division of labor has emerged between the two superpowers to fill in the system gap in world trade: while the Americans send the Soviet Union wheat and technical know-how, the Russians provide America with gas and have negotiated extensive investment agreements with the US in order to realize the most efficient use of the still vast and largely untouched store of Russian raw materials. American expertise plus American capital for Russian raw materials and energy supply—this seems to be the long term basis of an arrangement which is very likely to enlarge the limits to growth of the two largest independent industrial nations. It is quite evident that Japan, West Germany and other industrial states are also interested in joining in. We will examine the consequences which result in the following chapter.

The central question in this world economic and world political situation now arises: Are the industrial nations, especially the superpowers, in the position to broaden not only the growth potential for their economies through the concentrated application of their natural resources and their scientific-technical potential, but at the same time to improve the quality of growth significantly? Another question then arises as to whether this process will not succeed at the expense of the developing countries. It is clear that the industrial nations are not necessarily dependent upon the developing countries to attain this goal; on the contrary, they can increase the already existing nontariff restrictions through added duties and further limitations, thereby severely impairing the developing countries' export prospects. Johan Galtung points out this danger and goes so far as to maintain that the entire discussion of environmental protection and growth curtailment is primarily a concern of the rich countries, who, having attained a high material standard of living, now more than ever wish to impose limits to growth on other nations.[9] If it is true that the developed industrial nations are already straining the limits in the expansion of their scientific and technical activities up to now—limits to the environmental capacity to absorb pollutants and also limits to the availability of resources— then it follows that any rise in the material standard of living in the developing countries would be possible only at the expense of further economic growth in the industrialized countries. One can thus deduce an interest in the industrialized countries in hindering the economic growth of the developing countries.

The situation is not quite so simple, however. Both the generation of high quality growth within today's given boundaries and the expansion and complete utilization of the ecological system's capacity to absorb disturbances demand an extraordinarily intensive capital and research-oriented technology. Today only the most highly developed industrial nations have such facilities at their disposal. Physical limitations on resources do not pose the present problem; the fullest possible use or expansion of available space for adjustment does. The limited carrying capacity of the environment sets distinct limits and is in a broader sense the ultimate scarce good. The industrial nations will become less dependent upon supplies of raw materials from the developing countries to the degree that they are able to utilize the space available for adjustment, with the help of their advanced technology, and therefore be able to combine a high quality of growth with a high material standard of living. The near future will reveal how far the price increase due to the present scarcities in certain raw material markets will be able to compensate for the developing countries' other disadvantages. As we shall see below, this problem has already been investigated. These inter-relationships are illustrated in simplified form in Figure 1-5.

From a relatively high material standard of living, the industrial nations are striving toward a better quality of growth. This is represented by arrow 1. The developing countries, however, are still

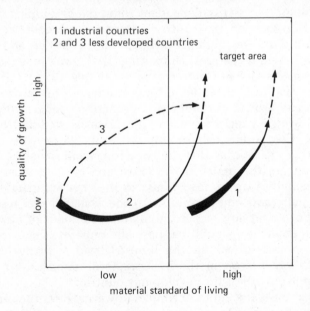

Figure 1-5.

at a relatively low material standard of living and must pursue an incomparably longer and more difficult path to attain both—namely, a rise in their material standard of living and at the same time an improvement in the quality of growth. According to conventional economic analysis, this can only occur by way of a temporary reduction of the material living standard. If one applies guidelines which are not strictly economic, there is a path toward development at least theoretically conceivable which places growth and living quality before a rise in the material standard of living. This possibility is represented by the dotted arrow 3. The industrial nations will hardly be ready, however, to restrict their own material standard of living in order to help the rise of the quality of growth in the developing nations. Yet the more the developing countries use their reserves of raw materials as a means of pressure, the more the industrial nations, independent of the ideological differences which might still separate them politically, will use their scientific-technical potential to serve a high quality growth conforming to the environment. The diagram's developmental path (3) is therefore a possibility for the developing countries only with the cooperation of the industrial nations. Along with this option one could imagine agreements similar to that between the USA and the Soviet Union today also emerging, *mutatis mutandis*, between the industrial nations on one side and at least some developing countries on the other. Countries with potential for such an arrangement would be primarily those who have already developed to a certain point and, most importantly, who have raw materials at their disposal—i.e., Brazil, Indonesia, India or Nigeria. Certain factors, to be explored in the following section, will determine whether or not an attempt to transform the worldwide competitive drive for growth into a developmental process compatible with the environment can be successful.

GROWTH LIMITATION VERSUS GROWTH DRIVE

One obvious indication of our current state of affairs is our inability to channel the processes of unlimited expansion in our technical and economic activities into the realm of a dynamic global equilibrium. Exponential growth in population, in the economy and thereby in the use of resources is, by definition, impossible in a closed system—and the earth, aside from the effects of solar radiation, must be considered as such. Men have learned to bring territories under their control; they have also developed a mastery over "structures." The Machine Age allowed man to devise new control systems and now the newest developments of space flight require mastery of the complex problem of the control over "man-machine-system." What we have not yet learned, however, is how to control the interaction between resource allocation, applied technologies, energy consumption, patterns of behavior and the effects of all these on the biosphere. In other words, the processes stemming from the interaction of the four subsystems to a large degree still elude our control today.

If one proceeds from the premise that any exponential growing process is, in a closed, finite system, impossible—and this is a logical necessity, at least in this abstract formulation—one immediately comes to the question of what kind of adjustment will occur. Is adjustment by collapse the most probable alternative, or can a continuous adjustment lead the way to a dynamic equilibrium? The answer depends, among other factors, upon the amount of time available to solve the problem. The nature of the exponential processes as well as the structure of feedbacks existing in a dynamic system of global interaction between the four subsystems shed light upon these questions.

The work done by Forrester and Meadows at the initiative of the Club of Rome, and later published under the now famous title *Limits to Growth*, led to at least two misunderstandings. The various simulation runs in Meadows' global model were treated as forecasts, and general blame was placed on the initiators of this concept—that is, on the Club of Rome—for their doomsday philosophy. Neither judgment is accurate, or at least not in such a generalized form. Forrester and Meadows pointed out themselves that their work in the area of the system dynamics theory did not deal with forecasts but was rather an attempt to clarify the dynamic behavior of such systems with the help of simulation techniques.[10]

Similar investigations had been carried out at MIT under the title "Industrial Dynamics"[a] as early as 1956.[11] When the book *Limits to Growth*[b] appeared, it was dismissed in many circles as alarmist tripe. One should also be wary of snap judgments here. With their popular version of the study, representatives of the Club of Rome really wanted only to draw the public's—and specifically the politicians'—attention to the global interrelationships, in the hope that this might result in some significant progress. The strategy of

[a]Jay W. Forrester, Industrial Dynamics, Cambridge, Mass. The M.I.T. Press, 1961.
[b]Dorella H. Meadows, Dennis L. Meadows et al., The Limits to Growth, Universe Books, New York, 1972.

this group is actually based on an optimism which maintains that the conditions for a continuous adjustment toward a supportable dynamic equilibrium still exist and an adjustment by collapse can thus be avoided.

What are the most important results of this systems dynamics approach? To begin with, it seems that some clarity has been achieved, at least in regard to the magnitudes of order of the time remaining before we reach the critical levels. All indexes show that we cannot continue for centuries of millenia as we have been; the time available to us for adjustment can be measured in decades. It seems, further, practically certain that technological environmental protection alone cannot lead us out of the danger zone of adjustment by collapse as long as (1) environmental stress is not concurrently reduced to zero discharge and/or (2) the exponential growth cannot be channeled into a zero growth process at a level compatible with the environment—a process which could temporarily produce negative growth rates in certain highly industrialized nations. It has become clear, too, that today one cannot examine the individual aspects of the economic, social, political and physical sectors of the environment separately from one another. One of the most outstanding characteristics of the Meadows study on the limits to growth, despite all the criticism which can be leveled at its incompleteness, is its ability to present the interaction of the different subsystems and their components in many positive and negative feedbacks and to make them reproducible at will through computer simulation. This analytical method achieves considerably more than the mental processing of individual causal connections or the accumulation of individual pieces of information on population growth, the economy, air or water pollution. That does not imply that this concept does not urgently require expansion and refinement. This is particularly true for the closer analysis of our planet's global energy balance and its inclusion into the world models. We know that heat pollution, an inevitable by-product of our use of energy, is the final inescapable pollution. It is therefore important to know to what extent we will be able to use solar radiation—an energy form which does not upset the planet's thermal balance with additional waste heat—as a substitute for the conventional energy we extract from fossil material or nuclear processes. The Meadows study must be further supplemented—and this is particularly urgent—by the incorporation of sociopolitical factors like education, mass communication, the degrees of participation, social mobility and the inequalities between nations. Work in this area has already begun. We will return to this research below.

Until now, no one has precisely formulated how an ecologically oriented economy should look in detail and in what way the transition from exponential growth to a constant, ecologically consistent level of activity could be effected under today's legal and political conditions. It is a fact that our competitive system, based on private industry, imposes an expansionary drive on the firms, which they cannot escape without sacrificing their existence. Whoever cannot expand—i.e., grow—will, over the short or long run, drop completely out of the market. On the other hand, it is by all means possible to achieve an improvement in human living conditions with a constant population and a constant supply of capital. John Stuart Mill pointed out this fact more than a hundred years ago.

For international comparison, seen from the perspective of these problems, one can divide the countries of the world into four categories: The first comprises countries which find themselves within an ecological equilibrium due to their low level of industrial-technical activity, but which still display an inadequate quality of growth. Most developing countries belong to this group. The second group stands in direct contrast to these countries; it consists of countries whose provision for social infrastructure is insufficient for what determines the quality of life, but which, in spite of, or perhaps due to, this fact, display a high and rising level of industrial-technical activity and therefore have a disturbed relation to the ecosystem. Prime examples are the USA, England and Japan. The third group includes countries whose social institutions guarantee a good quality of life, but whose high level of technical-industrial activity and lack of natural resources keep them from ecological equilibrium—i.e., Switzerland. The ideal situation is characterized by a high level of social infrastructure—i.e., a high quality of living—but at the same time, by a state of industrial-technical activity which would be, in the broadest sense, compatible with the environment. One might name New Zealand as an example here.

The initiators of the project "Predicament of Mankind" in the Club of Rome have stated the hope that the awareness of the factors which, following an "overshooting," would bring the possibility of adjustment by collapse threateningly close, could result in an international solidarity. If one considers, however, that the channeling of our world society from the unlimited drive for expansion into a situation of growth limitation compatible with the environment calls not only for a worldwide distribution of the already existing material sources, but also for an adjustment in the technical-economic activity levels of the various nations—and therefore, for example, sacrifices in growth by the rich industrial states—one cannot pin too many hopes on this solidarity effect. Every country and every organization will want to shift the inevitable costs of this adaptation onto the others. An intensification of the already existing competitive drive and a strengthening of the governmental structures in the international system seem therefore much more likely. The danger of a totally annihilating nuclear holocaust has become less probable, but we will have to face intensifying inter- and intranational conflicts instead. What consequences will follow internationally from growth limitation and what kind of growth limitation we will ultimately be dealing with are not questions of scientific understanding and international solidarity, but are, as all indexes substantiate, questions of power politics. The politics of the oil-producing countries leave no room for doubt on the subject.

Notes

1. See M. Basmanow, "Blinde Bomben," *Literaturnaja Gaseta*, no. 4, 4 April 1973. Allende could have been saved with 1,000 trucks and an economic assistance of four to five billion rubles; but how many "Cubas" can Russia afford in view of her engagement in the Middle East? Since the Russians have made the decision on their priorities, it seems likely that—at least in the near future—the revolutionary liberation movements in Latin America can not rely on any outside assistance.

2. See Johan Galtung, "The Limits to Growth and Class Politics" (Oslo: International Peace Research Institute, 1973), manuscript.

3. See A. Buchholz, *Wissenschaftlich-technische Revolution und Wettbewerb der Systeme, Osteuropa*, 22. Jg. H. (5 May 1972): 349.

4. The agreement between the United States of America and the Union of Soviet Socialist Republics, signed at Washington, June 21, 1973, makes explicit:

Reaffirming their conviction that the earliest adoption of further limitations of strategic arms would be a major contribution in reducing the danger of an outbreak of nuclear war and in strengthening international peace and security, the President of the United States of America, Richard Nixon, and the General Secretary of the Central Committee of CPSU, L.I. Brezhnev, have agreed as follows : *First.* The two sides will continue active negotiations in order to work out a permanent agreement on more complete measures on the limitation of strategic offensive arms, as well as their subsequent reduction, proceeding from the Basic Principles of Relations between the United States of America and the Union of Soviet Socialist Republics signed in Moscow on May 22, 1972, and from the Interim Agreement between the United States of America and the Union of Soviet Socialist Republics of May 26, 1972, on Certain Measures with Respect to the Limitation of Strategic Offensive Arms.

Over the course of the next year the two sides will make serious efforts to work out the provisions of the permanent agreement on more complete measures on the limitation of strategic offensive arms with the objective of signing it in 1974.

5. See John H. Adler, "Development and Income Distribution," *Finance and Development* 10, 3 (September 1973).

6. See R. Codoni, B. Fritsch, A. Melzer, F.J. Oertly, L. Sieber, and P. Walser, *World Trade Flows—Integrational Structure and Conditional Forecasts* (Zurich: Schulthess Polygraphischer Verlagae 1971).

7. See Lester R. Brown, "An Overview of World Trends," *The Futurist* VI, 6 (December 1972): 227.

8. See World Bank/IDA, Annual Report 1973, 93.

9. Galtung.

Chapter Two

The Structure of the
International System

THE ACTORS

The global ecological system conflicts with the formal sovereignty of the states. Serious problems of "buck passing" therefore result, problems which have been taken care of, up to now, by whoever was the most powerful. These power-oriented problems of responsibility avoidance are intensifying in conjunction with the emerging world ecology crisis. In order to appreciate the nature of these processes it is necessary to have a clear picture of the actors who are intimately involved with it (see Table 2-1).

One must form an idea of the wide spectrum of these actors. We are already aware of the great differences between the countries in

Table 2-1.

---

176 international governmental organizations (IGO)*
1620 international nongovernmental organizations (INGO)**
7276 multinational corporations (MNC)
135 nation states (1973)

9207 Actors

*In this group belong the organization of the UN family, the European Economic Community, etc.
**Such as organizations representing libraries, the press, documentation, churches, social sciences, law, trade unions, economics and finance, agricultural organizations, transport, sports etc.
The figures for the IGOs, INGOs, and the MNCs refer to 1970-1971.

Source: Yearbook of International Organizations, 13th ed. (Brussels: Union of International Associations) 1971, pp. 1007 ff.

size, population, population density, income per capita and other criteria. Let us take, for example, the difference in scale between Monaco's population of 23,000 and the People's Republic of China's 780 million, or between Monaco's dimensions, 1.9 square kilometers, and the USSR's 22.4 million square kilometers. The same spectrum exists in population density: Libya, Mauretania and Mongolia register one inhabitant per square kilometer, and Australia two; in contrast, Taiwan has 390, the Netherlands 319, and Monaco a startling 12,316. Per capita income ranges between $80 and nearly $5,000 (in Switzerland).

A comparison of some of the larger multinational firms with certain nation states is also interesting (compare the list of 20 of the largest multinational industrial firms in the world in Appendix C). A comparison of the total sales of the individual firms with certain nations' GNP produces the sequence in Table 2-2.

A comparison of the corporations' total sales and the GNP of the various countries represented here is not without its problems, since the firms mentioned also contribute to the countries' GNP. One can see, however, that large individual multinational corporations exhibit at least as great, if not greater, economic potential as many small and even medium-sized nation states. For example, the firms listed in Table 2-3 have representatives in more than 40 countries.

It is obvious that an unusually complex network results from the interaction of these actors and from their many-sided activities, a network that one can really no longer completely grasp in its en-

Table 2-2.

Corporations or nation states	Sales or Gross National Product respectively in millions of US dollars for 1970-71	Corporations or nation states	Sales or Gross National Product respectively in millions of US dollars for 1970-71
General Motors	28,264	Finland	11,210
Argentina	26,820	Norway	11,110
Belgium	26,320	Venezuela	10,210
Switzerland	20,850	General Electric	9,425
Standard Oil	18,701	Indonesia	8,880
South Africa	16,850	IBM	8,274
Ford Motor	16,433	Mobil Oil	8,243
Denmark	15,700	Chrysler	7,999
Austria	14,820	South Korea	7,910
Royal Dutch/Shell	12,734	Philippines	7,660

Table 2–3.

Farbwerke Hoechst AG	(43)
British Petroleum Company Ltd.	(52)
Empirial Chemical Industries Ltd.	(46)
The Shell Transport and Trading Co. Ltd.	(85)
Colgate/Palmolive Co.	(55)
Gulf Oil Corp.	(61)
ITT	(40)
Mobil Oil Corp.	(62)
NCR	(42)

*Figures in parentheses are the number of countries in which the firms are represented.

tirety. The following example will substantiate our contention. We have seen that there are 9,207 participants in the transnational system in 1970-1971. The number of possible connections between these members is 42,379,821. If, however, we want to take into account that the connection, for example, between a specific oil company and Venezuela is not without significance for the connection, say, between the United States and some Arab country, we then realize that a specific two-sided relationship between any partners can be significant to another relationship between any two partners. This produces an astounding number of cross-connections, namely 8.9×10^{14}. A mental exercise can illustrate how large this number is: If a computer were to require only one-tenth of a second for the comprehension, evaluation and storing of one pair of relations between each two participants, it would still take 2,848 years before the computer would be finished with its work.

It is therefore essential to narrow down the actual problem area through a number of preliminary decisions. There have been many practical, as well as theoretical, attempts to do just that, but we cannot examine them more closely here.[1] With the help of certain indicators, we will sift out a core group and contrast them with a peripheral group. It is only on this basis that we can demonstrate certain dependencies and important structures within the transnational system as well as investigate the question of how, if at all, we can engineer international, ecologically neutral growth.

For our first stage, we can conceive of the participants—that is, the government-related international organizations, the independent international organizations, the multinational corporations and the nations themselves—as the components which stand in relationship to each other as shown in Figure 2–1.

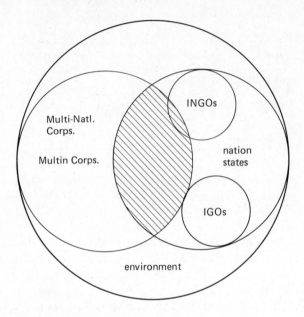

Figure 2-1.

As can be seen, the multinational companies overlap the so-called independent states in the areas of sovereignty and decisionmaking. The so-called IGOs and INGOs exist within the "nation" component. They merely touch the multinational companies' sphere of influence, not yet penetrating it, or perhaps not yet having been infiltrated by these companies. One must not forget, however, along with these four groups of actors, that there is a fifth player in this field of global interaction—the environment. The relationship of the actors to one another will be massively influenced by their relationships to the' environment.

THE CORE GROUP

If one examines these participants more closely, it becomes immediately clear that the economic and technological activities are concentrated in a very small central group of nations and multinational enterprises. One can see this plainly in the respective shares of the world GNP. In 1970 the world GNP amounted to $3,221.7 billion. From this total, Africa accounted for a mere 2.25 percent, Central and South America for 4.9 percent, Asia, excluding the

People's Republic of China, 5.19 percent, and the Pacific countries, including Australia, New Zealand and Papua, New Guinea, 1.4 percent. That is 13.74 percent altogether, which implies that the industrial nations of the world—that is, the United States, Canada, Western Europe, Eastern Europe, the USSR and Japan—generate 86.2 percent of the world GNP.

Let us go one step further and examine the most important industrial nations in the West and the socialist bloc more closely. The largest industrial nations adhering to the Western economic system are the United States, Canada, Great Britain, West Germany, France, Italy and Japan. The most highly industrialized nations in the Eastern bloc are the USSR, East Germany, Czechoslovakia, Poland and Hungary. If we put the economic potential of these 12 countries in 1970 together and express it as a percentage of the world total, the proportions which result are given in Table 2–4.

Let us now supplement this picture with a rank ordering of the top three and then the top six countries, using GNP, population and exports as criteria.

Table 2–5 presents each nation's share as a percentage of the world GNP, population and exports. Here it is also evident that, for example, 65.5 percent of the GNP in 1969 accrued to the USA, the USSR and Japan, West Germany, France and Great Britain. These same six countries accounted for 47.9 percent of world exports, but

Table 2–4.

	Percent of world total
GNP	74.04
Defense expenditures	82.37
Exports	60.58
Energy consumption	75.99
International liquidity (excluding socialistic countries for which no data are available)	54.87*
Capital formation	77.04

*International liquidity position = gold + special drawing rights + reserves at the IMF + convertible currency reserves.

Sources:

GNP: *World Bank Atlas 1972.*
Defense expenditures: *SIPRI Year Book 1972* (Stockholm, 1972).
Exports: *World Trade Flows*, (Zurich: Institute for Economic Research), 1971.
Energy consumption: *World Energy Supplies*, UN Statistical Papers, Series J, no. 15. 1972.
Intern. Liquidity: *UN Statistical Yearbook*, 1971.
Capital formation: *UN Statistical Yearbook*, and World Bank, World Tables 1972.

Table 2-5

Rank ordering 1969 and 1970	Gross National Product	Population	Exports
	Percent world total		
Gross National Product			
3 countries — USA, USSR, Japan	50.1 / 49.8	15.4 / 15.0	23.0 / 23.3
6 countries — Federal Republic of Germany, France, Great Britain	65.5 / 64.2	20.2 / 19.6	47.9 / 48.8
Population			
3 countries — China, India, USSR	15.5 / 19.0	43.0 / 44.0	2.8 / 2.3
6 countries — USA, Indonesia, Pakistan–Bangladesh	50.1 / 49.9	55.2 / 56.2	18.7 / 18.5
Exports			
3 countries — USA, Federal Republic of Germany, Great Britain	43.1 / 39.7	9.1 / 8.7	34.9 / 34.8
6 countries — Japan, France, Canada	56.8 / 53.2	14.0 / 13.5	52.3 / 53.6

only 20.2 percent of the world population. Forty-four percent of the world population lives in China, India and the USSR but, as the table shows, these countries account for a mere 2.3 percent of world exports.

A diagram like this clearly reveals the stratification of the international system. Even our selected group of multinational companies is very unevenly distributed. Of the 7,276 parent companies, 33.9 percent are located in the United States, 23.25 percent in Great Britain and 13.11 percent in West Germany. The differences become even clearer if one compares the number of country A's international corporations' branch offices in Country B with the number of B's corporations' branch offices in country A. As can be seen in Figure 2–2, American multinational firms in Luxembourg are 50 times more widely represented than their Luxembourg counterparts are in America. A further example shows the same trend: American multinational firms in Belgium are almost 26 times as widely represented as are Belgian firms in the United States. One can also see from this graph that, for example, France's multinational companies in Spain are better represented, relatively speaking, than the Dutch ones in Spain. As the graph shows, these asymmetries are very pronounced. There are, in addition, one-sided relationships—i.e., representatives of multinational companies in a developing country, when there are no corresponding agents from domestic firms in the developing country abroad.

The socialist countries are also included on a one-sided basis only in the network of multinational companies. Aside from certain official trade representatives in the West, the socialist industrial countries have no representatives of their industrial system nor any other direct participation in Western investment endeavours. A foreign-oriented "socialist multinational firm" would be a contradiction in terms. Marxist theorists stress that only the self-generating reproduction of capital underlying the private industry–oriented pursuit of profit induces companies to expand their markets beyond national boundaries. This very tendency will strengthen due to higher cost for environmental protection and the competitive struggle.

That is, however, only one way in which the economic-technical dynamics of the industrial nations are expressed. If one wishes to understand thoroughly the origins and consequences of the endogenic core process, one must begin with the premise that economic growth and technical research depend upon each other. The economic use of new technical discoveries is not only a prerequisite, but is, at the same time, an impetus to developments of new production technologies, because these technologies alone offer enterprises a real chance to survive the competitive struggle. We are aware today that

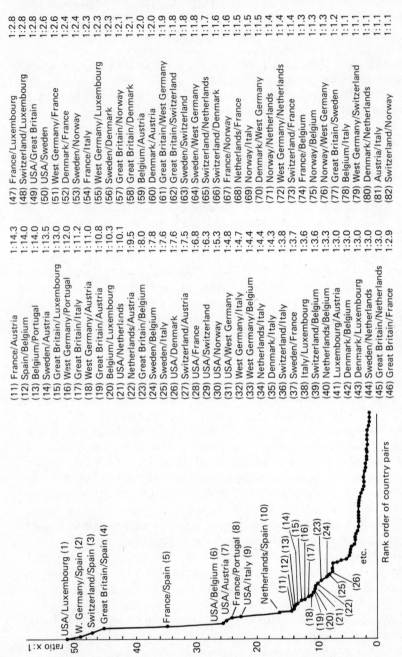

(1) USA/Luxembourg
(2) W. Germany/Spain
(3) Switzerland/Spain
(4) Great Britain/Spain
(5) France/Spain
(6) USA/Belgium
(7) USA/Austria
(8) France/Portugal
(9) USA/Italy
(10) Netherlands/Spain

(11) France/Austria	1:14.3	
(12) Spain/Belgium	1:14.0	
(13) Belgium/Portugal	1:14.0	
(14) Sweden/Austria	1:13.5	
(15) Great Britain/Luxembourg	1:13.0	
(16) West Germany/Portugal	1:13.0	
(17) Great Britain/Italy	1:11.2	
(18) West Germany/Austria	1:11.0	
(19) Great Britain/Austria	1:10.8	
(20) Belgium/Luxembourg	1:10.3	
(21) USA/Netherlands	1:10.1	
(22) Netherlands/Austria	1:9.5	
(23) Great Britain/Belgium	1:8.0	
(24) Sweden/Belgium	1:7.8	
(25) Sweden/Italy	1:7.6	
(26) USA/Denmark	1:7.6	
(27) Switzerland/Austria	1:7.5	
(28) USA/France	1:6.8	
(29) USA/Switzerland	1:6.3	
(30) USA/Norway	1:5.3	
(31) USA/West Germany	1:4.8	
(32) West Germany/Italy	1:4.7	
(33) West Germany/Belgium	1:4.4	
(34) Netherlands/Italy	1:4.4	
(35) Denmark/Italy	1:4.3	
(36) Switzerland/Italy	1:3.8	
(37) Sweden/France	1:3.7	
(38) Italy/Luxembourg	1:3.6	
(39) Switzerland/Belgium	1:3.6	
(40) Netherlands/Belgium	1:3.3	
(41) Luxembourg/Austria	1:3.3	
(42) Denmark/Belgium	1:3.0	
(43) Denmark/Luxembourg	1:3.0	
(44) Sweden/Netherlands	1:3.0	
(45) Great Britain/Netherlands	1:3.0	
(46) Great Britain/France	1:2.9	

(47) France/Luxembourg	1:2.8	
(48) Switzerland/Luxembourg	1:2.8	
(49) USA/Great Britain	1:2.8	
(50) USA/Sweden	1:2.6	
(51) West Germany/France	1:2.6	
(52) Denmark/France	1:2.4	
(53) Sweden/Norway	1:2.4	
(54) France/Italy	1:2.3	
(55) West Germany/Luxembourg	1:2.3	
(56) Sweden/Denmark	1:2.3	
(57) Great Britain/Norway	1:2.1	
(58) Great Britain/Denmark	1:2.1	
(59) Belgium/Austria	1:2.0	
(60) Denmark/Austria	1:2.0	
(61) Great Britain/West Germany	1:1.9	
(62) Great Britain/Switzerland	1:1.8	
(63) Sweden/Switzerland	1:1.8	
(64) Sweden/West Germany	1:1.8	
(65) Switzerland/Netherlands	1:1.7	
(66) Switzerland/Denmark	1:1.6	
(67) France/Norway	1:1.6	
(68) Netherlands/France	1:1.5	
(69) Norway/Italy	1:1.5	
(70) Denmark/West Germany	1:1.5	
(71) Norway/Netherlands	1:1.4	
(72) West Germany/Netherlands	1:1.4	
(73) Switzerland/France	1:1.4	
(74) France/Belgium	1:1.4	
(75) Norway/Belgium	1:1.3	
(76) Norway/West Germany	1:1.3	
(77) Great Britain/Sweden	1:1.3	
(78) Belgium/Italy	1:1.2	
(79) West Germany/Switzerland	1:1.1	
(80) Denmark/Netherlands	1:1.1	
(81) Austria/Italy	1:1.1	
(82) Switzerland/Norway	1:1.1	

Rank order of country pairs

ratio x:1   50   40   30   20   10   0

Source: Werner J. Feld, Nongovernmental Forces and World Politics, Praeger, New York, 1972, p. 30.

approximately 80 percent of the real growth of an industrially developed economic system is attributable to technical advancement and only 20 percent to a more rational utilization of the factors of production. The functions of basic research have now changed to the degree that the results of applied science have become significantly greater for the competing enterprises. Although pure research still exists in principle, it has become more closely connected with economic and general corporate concerns, a situation due in part to the sharply rising costs. During the process of accelerating development of production powers following the end of World War II, pure basic research—l'art pour l'art, so to speak—became impossible. This change had far-reaching consequences, both for the individual scientists and for the relationship between the state economy and science in the industrial nations. By this time, on the one hand, the responsibility of the scientists involved with basic research was also becoming more and more obvious. On the other hand, the state could no longer limit itself to financing science functioning in an ivory tower, while the economy was beginning to organize basic research on a large scale adapted to its needs.

The new forms of cooperation developed since then within the strategic triangle of state-science-economy have proven to be both extraordinarily effective and dangerous, as became clear in the space research in the USA. One can observe two main trends in the development of the mutual influences of state, economy and sciences on each other:

1. As the activity level rises, an increasing interweaving of societal and technical phenomena results, in which the complexity and accompanying vulnerability to disturbances increases sharply (and is still increasing), particularly in the scientific and capital intensive sectors of the industrial societies.[2]
2. The forces set loose in this triangular relationship produce an accelerating autogenic expansion of economic growth, consuming resources and energy, which means that, in certain spheres and soon on a global scale, both ecological and societal-political stress limits will be reached.

The outward results of these two trends are increasing conflict between the demand (preprogrammed up to now with advertising) for more consumer goods, which implies an added rise in wages, and the possibility—a limited one today—to do justice to the suggestions made to combat environmental problems—for example, extra cost increases for environmental protection as a result of the general application of the so-called pay as you pollute principle (PPP), whereby each enterprise is responsible for the elimination and prevention of environmental stresses caused by its activities.

Other less positive results might be increasing pressure on the profit margin, more intense competition, rising specialization, broadening multinational firms, increasing social conflicts and rising inflation. These problems affecting the state, science and economy at a relatively high technological-economic level dominate the Western sector of the industrial core group, in particular, today. They do not continue a linear development with increased expansion of productive forces, however; instead they come under the influence of opposing forces, which forces begin to work more and more strongly as the limits to this process of expansion become more distinct. These opposing forces reveal themselves in the political actualization of *new goals and priorities:*[3]

1. Economic growth, as such, will no longer unreservedly be regarded as the top priority in the Western industrial nations.
2. State interference in the market mechanism will become increasingly unavoidable. It will express itself, among other methods, in measures to internalize external costs (application of the pay as you pollute principle through duties, taxes, etc.) as well as, to some extent, in direct price and wage controls.
3. Direct state participation in the preparation of those goods—particularly collective goods—and services, which, due to the characteristics of the market mechanism, cannot be supplied in enough quantity, if at all, by the private economy. The following belong to this category:

   the social infrastructure;
   regional planning;
   new local public transportation systems;
   establishment of social and preventative medicine;
   educational systems, particularly adult education;
   hospitals, rest homes;
   consumer protection;
   research planning, innovative research, etc.

During the past three decades, these problems have been added to the traditional governmental tasks of guaranteeing internal and external security (legal and defense). The function of the government therefore becomes extraordinarily complex, particularly in relation to science and the economy. One should not forget, however, that the "market economy" system materialized in a very short time period—namely, from about 1871–1914. Before then there was a "political economy." Today we find ourselves in the midst of a process which has long since abandoned the principle of a pure market economy and is heading in the direction of a "political economy of a higher order" in which more—and more significant—decisions will be made through *political* institutions, not through the market mechanism.

The market mechanism does not release us from the necessity, however unpleasant, of deciding *what kind* of growth we want to have, *how* it should be socially structured, what models of urbanization and settlements we wish to emulate, etc.

The necessity for such political decisions in developed industrial societies has not only become more pressing to the extent that the areas in which market economy processes function automatically have shriveled, but also due to the fact that the *dangers* accompanying this development have become greater. The more the expansion of all productive forces accelerates, the greater will be the number of humans who "drop out" of this process, not only as unemployed in the realm of "structural employment" as it is known in economic jargon, but also in a much more profound sense. Even when they wish to work, many people cannot muster the emotional strength to cope with the changes in this process of continually accelerating development. People are overwhelmed by the technical, social and political innovations and are relegated to an existence of bitterness, pent-up aggression or dejected hopelessness, often before they reach 60. It is in this manner that the totally rationalized industrial process begets continually changing peripheral groups as a kind of by-product. The thoroughly rationalized process designed to supply people with material goods thus is continually producing new irrationality and resulting in the dropping out of those who become alienated from all material security offered by the total rationality of the industralization process.

This development can lead to situations where the capacity of the political regulative powers historically at our disposal within the institutions is overstrained. The still rising wave of blackmail reveals not only the huge vulnerability of our complex industriosocietal system, but also the inability of our societal institutions to rid themselves of this disease.

We have seen that our industrialization process must avoid not only new environmental damage, but must also repair the damages already incurred. This simply means that in the near future the industrial nations will not be able to count on the same rate of increase in the material standard of living, at least as it is now defined. It follows, then, that millions of discontented people will be added to the above-mentioned peripheral groups, because they won't comprehend why an improvement in the material standard of living possible ten years ago is no longer possible today. That and much more impairs the political regulative powers of the core group—powers which are vital for the process of transition from the quantitative growth we have experienced up to now to the new forms of qualitative growth. Because the core group countries have a much higher material level of activity than the developing countries do, they pose a real threat to the periphery, since the dwindling regulative powers can be compensated for a time by this group's ability to shift burdens onto others. The ability to solve problems and to shift unpleasant adjustment difficulties onto another are like communicating arteries: the larger the adjustment difficulties in transition from quantitative to qualitative growth, and the larger the inner impairment of the political regulative powers, the greater the temptation to employ the not insignificant potential for "buck passing" to deal with the inner difficulties.

The situation is different in the socialist industrial nations. There one must follow a "catch up" policy, as the backwardness of their computer technology compared to the West's clearly illustrates, but one can do this for now without any consideration of negative side effects, since traces of pollution are not yet detectable, for example, in the vast reaches of the Soviet Union. This explains why the priorities in the socialist countries are still oriented toward the original goals of immediate industrialization: production of more investment goods, more consumer goods, improvement of technical and life standards, etc. These nations will, however, soon experience the problems which are so acute for us today. For this reason, a strengthened cooperation between the two sociopolitical factions within the core group of industrial nations will, as it to some degree already has, result. One can infer that one part of the technical-economic powers of the core group will be directed eventually at overcoming the negative effects of thoughtless, purely economically based growth. Our thesis states that the core countries will have much larger opportunities to accomplish this than the developing countries will, and that the priority given to handling these problems will result in new scientific powers, potentially at the expense of the developing countries. The kind of technology necessary to solve the problems of the postindustrial society is fundamentally different from the technology to be used in solving the developing countries' problems. An increasing asymmetry and incongruence has developed between the needs of the international firms transferring their technology to the developing countries and the technology appropriate to the developing countries' problems. This inconsistency is of minor interest to most multinational firms, however.

One should keep the order of magnitude in view when speaking of the economic-technical strength in the core countries. Canada's GNP, for example, at $79.1 billion in 1970, is larger than the combined GNPs of all the African nations put together, including South Africa's which was only $72.6 billion in 1970. Such comparisons reveal the potential which has already developed through the self-strengthening dynamics of the core group and which will undoubtedly develop further at a very high scientific level with the emergence of new technologies. If one considers a nation's percentage share of territory, taking resources into consideration, as a component of its potential power, and adds to that the other percentages of world totals in defense expenditure—GNP and population—one can draw up a rank ordering according to each nation's power potential (see Table 2–6). India, Brazil, Australia and Mexico all have a place in this schema, a fact which might be very significant for the future relations between the core group and the less potentially powerful countries of the Third World.

Table 2–6. Components of the Power Potential—Defense Expenditures, Population, GNP and Land Area (in percentages of respective world totals)

Country	Percent of total defense expenditures	Percent of world population	Percent of world product	Percent of land area of all nation states	Average
USA	38.70	5.59	30.28	7.01	20.37
USSR	27.80	6.63	13.59	16.77	16.12
China	5.21	23.84	3.78	7.16	10.00
India	0.85	14.71	1.78	2.45	4.95
Canada	1.03	0.58	2.46	7.47	2.89
Brazil	0.28	2.54	1.19	6.37	2.63
West Germany	2.97	1.68	5.60	0.19	2.62
Japan	0.57	2.83	6.17	0.03	2.46
France	2.98	1.39	4.89	0.41	2.41
Great Britain	3.00	1.52	3.93	0.18	2.16
Australia	0.60	0.34	1.10	5.75	1.95
Italy	1.11	1.47	2.94	0.23	1.44
Mexico	0.11	1.38	1.05	1.48	1.01
Poland	1.44	0.90	1.43	0.23	1.00
Argentina	0.21	0.63	0.83	2.08	0.94

THE PERIPHERAL GROUP

There are more than a hundred countries in the peripheral group that function at an astoundingly low level of technical and scientific activity. Although the comparison of GNPs has only a limited validity, it does provide certain points of reference, especially when one is dealing with large scale differences. Ninety-eight percent of all the funds set aside for research and development are provided and spent by the industrial nations. Seventy percent of the world population lives in the developing countries, yet they produce only 13.7 percent of the world product, and the remaining 30 percent who live in the industrial nations produce a total of 84.3 percent of the world product. The developing countries have a much lower activity level and a much more limited capacity to solve problems, especially when faced with those occasioned by the industrial nations' economic drives. These countries' own problems, measured against those of the industrial nations, are in no way easier to solve—quite the contrary.

It would be inappropriate to give an exhaustive analysis of the developing countries' problems here, since numerous studies have already been published on the subject.[4] One should at least outline the most important problem areas, however.

First of all, there is the *problem of population:* 25 countries (see Appendix No. 8) show a yearly population increase of 3 percent or more. These 25 countries thus represent approximately 8 percent of the world population. *Unemployment* and *malnutrition* are also on the increase. The Green Revolution, as many investigations predicted, created more problems than it solved. It led to disturbances of the ecological equilibrium, destroyed social structures, aggravated the inequalities between the poor and the wealthy farmers, did not fundamentally improve the nutritional situation and, finally, had no braking effect on the population growth. These are only a sampling of the effects which the Green Revolution has had; today it seems that our next step must be to learn to live with these new conditions and to incorporate them into the process of social development.

Life expectancy in these countries lags far behind that of the industrial nations. According to a 1972/73 study by the World Health Organization, in the last eight years the average life expectancy in the developing countries has risen from 41.7 to 49.6 years. West Africa has the shortest average life expectancy: it rose from 32.5 years in 1950 to only 39.2 years by 1970. Let us contrast that statistic with the average life expectancy of about 70 years in the industrial countries.

Inequalities in *income distribution* have become greater, both within and between the various countries. Here we are dealing with the contradiction between growth and social justice. No one has yet succeeded in combining increasing growth rates with more equitable income distribution. Due to this fact, the wide discrepancies in income between the individual developing countries are also reflected in their domestic situations. During the second "development decade," 25 countries were singled out as being the least developed, economically speaking. The criteria included a per capital income of under $100, a degree of industrialization amounting to less than 10 percent and, finally, an illiteracy level, derived from all inhabitants over 15, of 80 percent or more.

The 25 countries include Africa's Botswana, Burundi, Chad, Dahomey, Ethiopia, Guinea, Lesotho, Mali, Malawi, Niger, Ruwanda, Somalia, Sudan, Tanzania, Uganda and Upper Volta; in Asia and the Pacific, Afghanistan, Bhutan, Laos, the Maledives, Nepal, Sikkim, West Samoa and Yemen; and finally, in Latin America, Haiti. India, Indonesia and Pakistan come close to fitting this definition and Bangladesh clearly falls into the category. It was not included only because it had not been recognized as an independent nation at the time of the study.

These striking inequalities between the developing nations combined with the increasing social tensions within the individual countries are, on the one hand, the expression, and on the other, the consequence of numerous interlocking negative feedbacks. For instance, the level of income is low because productivity is poor; poor productivity results from the people's poor physical condition and this problem relates directly back to the low income level, leaving us exactly where we started. Here is one further example: The illiteracy level is very high because there are no schools. No schools can be built because there are no investment funds. There can be no investment funds because the income level is too low, and that situation stems from the population's lack of education. This process has once again brought us to the beginning of the problem.

Developmental strategy attempts, among other things, to break through these vicious circles. This is not always easy, since blocking off one extraneous problem results in the creation of another. Let us take the relationship between economic growth and foreign trade as an example. If we try to equalize the differences in growth levels and to realize higher growth rates in each country with a low income level, we generally will end up increasing the import surplus in those countries whose growth we have stimulated. This merely substitutes the problem of increasing inequality in the balance of trade for the problem of differences in the growth rate.

One of the many sources of the developing countries' difficulties is the unequal distribution of international developmental aid. As can be seen from Figure 2-3, the smaller countries receive a relatively high per capita share of foreign aid, while the larger nations—populationwise—receive a much smaller per capita share. This has led to successful development within the smaller countries, while the large countries, like Indonesia, India and Brazil, have developed more slowly in comparison to their more fortunate neighbors. Mexico is an exception to this rule because it long ago reached the point where independent economic development was possible, and therefore requires less developmental aid today.

How do the governments of the developing countries, on the one hand, and those of the industrial countries, on the other, react to these difficulties? Let us first try to uncover a few crucial aspects of the strategy of developmental policy similar to that outlined by McNamara, president of the World Bank. The main emphasis of the new strategy today, as McNamara specified, is on the struggle against so-called *absolute poverty*. The victims are 40 percent of the poorest people in a country composed mainly of small farmers. It is the rural

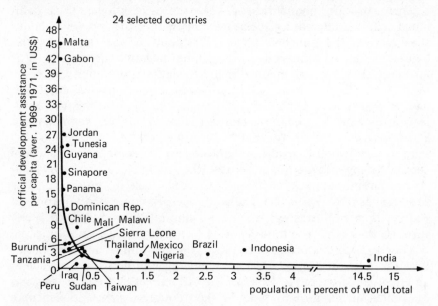

Figure 2-3.

poverty which is a major priority problem in developmental policy today and which should be combatted with massive financial aid. This strategy attempts to fight against the increasing inequalities of income within the countries while preventing more people from migrating to the overcrowded cities. An agricultural program which seeks to achieve a yearly 5 percent production expansion from the small farmers, starting in 1985, stands in the center of this strategy. Prerequisites for the success of this program include an acceleration in agrarian and land reforms, as well as a change in the social structures. It is the latter which lies outside of the World Bank's sphere of influence, a fact which McNamara clearly pointed out.

The second thrust of the seventies' international development strategy concentrates on the 25 poorest countries which we have already named. During the second development decade they should receive special support by being offered credit at low interest rates and generous terms. Finally, technology transfer to the developing countries should be systematically encouraged. The important role of the multinational corporations in this connection is apparent. On the other hand, one must also recognize that these corporations will primarily transfer a technology serving their purposes, and will not necessarily pass on every piece of information which is important to the developing countries. The core group would, in principle, have to concentrate part of their scientific-technical potential on the development and transfer of developmentally oriented technologies. There would be certain advantages to proceeding in this fashion. First of all, the transfer of technology, as a rule, does not directly burden the trade balance or the balance of payments. Second, the effects on the developmental process are more permanent than those resulting from traditional financial help, which often falls flat precisely because there is no qualified personnel to make use of the requisite technical information and the managerial know-how.

The total developmental strategy today is therefore concentrated on creating conditions designed to fulfill the basic needs of the developing countries within a reasonable time. Calculations have shown, however, that much more capital than has previously been available will be necessary, even for this relatively modest goal. If one wished to raise the general standard of living in the developing countries to the equivalent of $500 per capita within ten years, one would need about $600 billion, or $60 billion per year, having taken into consideration today's rate of population growth and the growth rate of the productivity of capital in the current technical level of development. We are presently transferring a nominal $17 billion per year.

It will therefore be possible to achieve a generally acceptable standard of living within the next ten to 15 years only if we substantially raise the amount of developmental aid, encourage the transfer of development-oriented technologies and bring population growth under control. These three requirements cannot, however, be met overnight, for both political and technical reasons.

How do the nations in the "peripheral group" react to the developmental policy's limited success? To begin with, there is strong prejudice against Western culture. Many countries protest against the relics of European civilization and decadence. They search for their own patterns of development, often ending up with uncritically adopting the Chinese example as their model. These countries' elite, however, often find themselves in a dilemma. On the one hand, they have adopted the Western ideals and values, have a Western lifestyle and think in terms similar to those of their Western colleagues, with whom they have studied in the same universities in the Western industrial countries. On the other hand, they can clearly see that the gulf between their expectations and the possibilities for their realization is widening. To avoid the inevitable political danger, this elite propagates anti-West, pro-Chinese ideology, often against its private convictions, while accepting Western development aid.

In this section we have spoken of the developing countries as a peripheral group. This is an accurate label only in relation to the potential for power which can be detected behind the economic and technical differences between the countries. Otherwise, one can hardly label the developing countries as a whole a peripheral group, although one of the most distinguished experts on development, Raoul Prebisch, himself coined the term "periphery" in connection with the developing countries and spoke of an increasing movement toward the periphery. It is only in this context that I have used the term.

The question now arises as to what the developing countries expect from the future. They do not seem to be in a position to solve the problems briefly outlined above. The entire problem of international growth, particularly the demand for clean growth, has created extra problems for the developing countries. On the one hand they see their vulnerability to the threat of restrictions, which the industrial nations could set up against the developing countries' export production for environmental protection reasons. On the other hand, the developing countries are also in danger of becoming a kind of garbage dump for the developed industrial nations' pollution industries. If one insisted upon the strict standards of a clean quality growth from the beginning of the industrialization process in the developing countries, one would thereby drastically slow down the growth process and further delay the urgently required fulfillment of their basic needs. There is therefore a connection between the development of the self-generating dynamics within the core group of industrial nations and the development possibilities of the Third World. If one examines the total gamut of all economic and scientific activities, one ends up concluding that almost all the problems existing in connection with growth limitation can be solved within the core group, i.e., without any participation from the developing countries. If this conclusion is correct, the developing countries could be faced with the danger that the industrial nations could virtually ignore the destiny of the Third World.

GRAVITATIONAL FIELDS OF POWER

Gravitational fields of power will be activated when existing dependencies become menaces. There are complementary dependencies which, in the sense of comparative cost advantages, give each partner certain advantages. On the other hand, there are the dependencies which limit individual options and then turn into situations where one partner totally dominates the relationship.

Let us touch upon the dependencies in the military and economic areas and point out the resulting political consequences. For this purpose we will use a simplified representation of the most important relationships between the major participants (see Figure 2–4).

Although it would be very tempting to consider the world pentagonal—that is, as a system of dependencies basically dominated by five forces—a more or less realistic examination requires the addition of more factors. Our diagram uses a total of 14 actors or regions. There is a maximum of 91 two-sided relationships between them, as well as 4,095 secondary relationships—i.e., relationships between relationships. We have reproduced only 29 of these relationships in our diagram. We have come much closer to reality, however, than the still widely used pentagonal world model can. Nine of the actors are in the Northern Hemisphere and five—namely, Latin America, Africa, Southeast Asia, Pakistan and India—are in the Southern Hemisphere. Eighty-two and four-tenths percent of the world defense expenditure is made by the industrial nations in the Northern Hemisphere, from whom the force fields of power emanate. The military-political situation is completely dominated by the major powers' nuclear monopoly. This is how the pentagonal world model—comprised of the USA, the USSR, Great Britain, France and China—was derived. If one wants to give economic factors a world

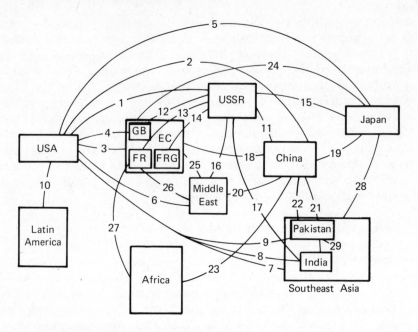

Figure 2-4.

role, the organization of the simplified pentagonal model must change: China must be replaced by Japan and France by West Germany. It is already clear what problems can arise using this model.

Moreover, the nuclear monopoly of the big powers is disintegrating. It is estimated that the process of economic development in the industrial nations will produce at least 15 countries who will have tactical atomic weapons at their disposal by 1980. In this connection it must be pointed out that neither France nor China has signed the Nonproliferation Treaty. We cannot examine the extremely complicated relationships between the atomic powers with regard to the structure and development of their nuclear armament. The facts are clear, however. Despite the Soviet-American détente, already mentioned, the situation is highly unstable and has not yet resulted in any limitation on quantitative and qualitative improvements in atomic defense systems.

A growing intensification of international competition looms in the economic sector, due to more expensive raw materials, the rise in wage costs and the added burdens placed on enterprises in Western industrial nations by the "Pay as you Pollute principle." This will result in concentration and further expansion of the multinational firms as well as a trend toward transferring production facilities to areas with cheaper work forces—i.e., primarily to those regions of the Third World which pose no large political risks for big business. Such regions include Singapore, Indonesia and Hong Kong, as well as many Latin American countries.

A large part of the funds earmarked for new product development, the push for new markets and advertising must now be channeled into the investigation of production processes which are more friendly to the environment and into new recycling technology. As a result of these massive cost increases, only a few giant enterprises can cope with these difficulties; the reasons for the trend toward concentration and internationalization are clear. As the table in Appendix G.4 indicates, the share of world trade from the Western industrial nations rose from 66.75 percent in 1961-1965 to almost 72 percent in 1971. In the aftermath of the oil crisis this trend was partly reversed.

If one combines the Western and socialistic industrial countries, then the share of world exports rises to 81 percent in 1971. Yet studies show that the relative level of intensity of export trade between the industrial nations has not yet uniformly reached the levels of the prewar period.[5] One can therefore surmise that these nations' relative share of world trade will increase even further.

It would be a mistake, however, to gloss over the basic differences between these two groups of industrial nations. It is exactly these divergent interests which will permit a sound basis for exchange between the Western industrial nations and the so-called socialist economic systems for the new few years. While the socialist industrial nations are still experiencing the classical industrial boom, and, moreover (this is particularly true for Russia), have a virtually unlimited supply of raw materials at their disposal, the Western industrial nations are becoming increasingly conscious of their environment—a phenomenon intimately connected with problems already experienced, particularly in overcrowded areas. In this situation the problem of the supply of raw material is of immediate interest, especially to the European industrial countries. In spite of its minimal dependence on foreign trade, the United States must also count on imports of raw materials, however. It is not surprising, therefore, that the Western industrial nations are so interested in a cooperative agreement with the Soviet Union and offer technical expertise as well as shipments of grain and other agricultural products in exchange for raw materials. The danger zone in this situation, however, is the Western industrial nations' large dependence upon oil from the

Middle East. If we transfer Table 2–6's power potential index to the horizontal axis and let the vertical axis represent raw oil imports as a percentage of domestic energy needs (having deducted the export of any refined products) we obtain another ranking of the nations of the world (see Figure 2–5). It becomes obvious that countries like the People's Republic of China, Russia (at that time still a net oil exporter) and the USA, which have large power potentials, are not particularly dependent on raw oil imports, while the countries with a limited power potential display a large dependence. There is, however, a "middle group" consisting of Brazil, West Germany, Great Britain, Australia and Canada which, in contrast to Japan and Italy, have the chance to reduce their dependence on oil from the Middle East either through diversification of domestic energy sources or the exploitation of domestic energy reserves.

The energy situation's dimensions are formidable. According to several experts, the United States will require $18–24 billion by 1980 for its energy imports.* By 1980, Japan will need the equivalent of $12–16 billion, while Europe's energy import bill will be between $23–31 billion. Total foreign exchange requirements by these countries—centers of consumption—will run to between $50–70 billion yearly.[6]

Compare these figures with the foreign exchange earnings of the oil-producing countries. The OPEC countries' yearly profits from exporting petroleum totaled $2.8 billion in 1962, $7.65 billion in 1970 and approximately $15.0 billion in 1972. On the basis of pre-1973 prices and dollar parity, earnings are estimated at $20 billion for 1975 and at approximately $50–55 billion for 1980. By the mid-1980s, the total volume of available foreign exchange reserves accumulating in the oil-producing countries should amount to $150–200 billion.

What will the oil-producing countries do with these huge sums? Three areas of use have been outlined, the first being investment at home. Only some of the oil-producing countries—for example, Iran, Algeria and Libya—can take advantage of this possibility. Investment in Western industrial nations, in particular the United States, is the second possibility. Limits have been placed on this alternative, however, since no one wants a large proportion of Western industry under the control of the oil-producing countries. The final way of using the funds involves keeping at least some of them in the form of liquid assets. This last alternative would pose an added danger to the

*These figures are based upon the pre-1973 oil price level.

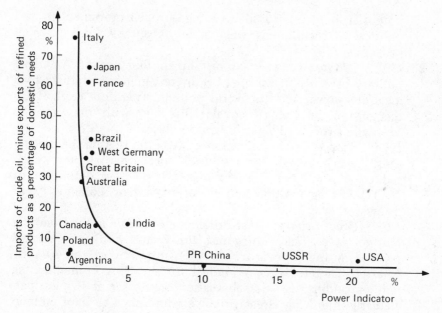

Figure 2-5.

international monetary system; by the end of this century the oil-producing countries will probably be in the position to sabotage any reforms in the international monetary system which may have been achieved. It follows unequivocally that problems and dangers to the international system which cannot be overlooked have resulted from the Western industrial countries' heavy dependence on oil imports and from the effects of this on both the oil-producing and oil-importing countries. The developing countries will hardly profit from the situation, although Peru, Ecuador, Thailand, Burma and Indonesia, along with countries like Nigeria and Venezuela that are already in the oil business, will be able to increase their oil exports sharply in the coming years. In this connection, it is interesting to note that UNCTAD, as the respresentative of the developing countries' interests, demanded lower prices on oil imports. The oil-producing countries promptly refused this request.

Let us conclude by returning once more to the relationships reproduced in Figure 2-4. They can be paraphrased as follows:

1. *USA - USSR:* Unstable nuclear balance, increased cooperation in economic areas; exchange of technical know-how for raw materials; growing interest by Moscow in American economic

potential; joint interest in impeding Europe's movement toward political unification as well as in expanding joint research programs.

2. *USA - China:* Chinese interest in continuance of American military presence in Europe; US interest in incorporating China into the power play in world politics. Therefore explicit US recognition of China's equal rights and with that a more prestigious role for Peking in world politics.

3. *USA - Europe:* New definition of Atlantic relationships including Japan's; search for a solution for burden sharing, troop reductions, monetary arrangements, etc. New definition of NATO strategy within the realm of a new community of interest.

4. *USA - Great Britain:* Great Britain's special role in the Common Market as possible protagonist for France and as important partner in the process of the reorganization of the Atlantic Charter. Therefore major interest for the USA in maintaining and expanding the special relationship to Great Britain, particularly following Great Britain's admittance to the Common Market.

5. *USA - Japan:* US interest in reducing trade imbalances with Japan; new definition of the partnership relationship between Japan and the US; new forms of multinational cooperation in the area of industrial development and research.

6. *USA - oil-producing countries:* In the short run, rising dependence on Middle East oil. In the long run, massive efforts to reduce this dependence, direct conflict of interest between US dependence upon oil from the Middle East and pro-Israel policy, development of additional options through the establishment of special relationship with Iran; possibility of direct intervention in acute crises not out of the question.

7. *USA - Southeast Asia:* US military disengagement; development of economic relations with Indonesia; competitive relationship with Japan in this region.

8. *USA - India:* Impairment of American-Indian relationships due to Soviet-Indian friendship pact as well as Soviet support of India in India-Pakistan conflict. The USA is nevertheless important for India, economically speaking.

9. *USA - Pakistan:* Strategic importance of Pakistan in struggle for spheres of influence in the Indian Ocean; therefore close connections with the USA and possible parallel interests with China.

Pakistani interest in establishment of counterbalance to India's predominance.

10. *USA - Latin America:* No official further development of the original goals of the "Alliance for Progress," but further strengthening of the dominance relationship in the economic area. No active impairment of this policy by the Soviet Union, increasing importance of the multinational corporations; only slim chance of success for the liberation movements due to lack of support by the Soviet Union.

11. *USSR - China:* Presently characterized by military motives; approximately half of the 4,000 mile long frontier between the two nations is disputed. New role for China in struggle against Soviet "social imperialism," exposure of Soviet interests in the Mediterranean and the Indian Ocean by China; China's resistance to Soviet claims of dominance.

12. *European Economic Community (Common Market) - USSR:* Moscow's rapprochements toward the EEC, establishment of official connections between the EEC and COMECON, incorporation of economic factors into the Soviet policy of détente; Soviet interest in exploiting the economic potential of the EEC for the purpose of modernizing its own economy.

13. *France - USSR:* Here, too, French efforts to receive special treatment from the Soviet Union with the idea of strengthening its position in the EEC. Soviet interest in France's role despite official recognition of the EEC.

14. *USSR - West Germany (FRG):* German interest in further development of economic, industrial and technical cooperation with the Soviet Union; construction of industrial facilities by West Germany in the Soviet Union; exchange of patents, licenses, know-how and technical information; German participation in the development of Siberian resources; scientific-technical cooperation in the area of environmental protection; Soviet interest in bilateral cooperative arrangements with Germany outside the EEC.

15. *USSR - Japan:* Decrease in Japan's relative share of foreign trade with the communist countries; Japanese interest in exploitation of Siberian deposits of raw materials and in Russian oil supplies; Russian interest in Japanese investment and know-how.

16. *USSR - oil-producing countries:* Soviet interest in friendly relations with the oil-producing countries, particularly due to

Western Europe's massive dependence on oil imports from the Middle East; Arab interest in shipment of weapons from the Soviet Union for their fight against Israel.

17. *USSR - India:* Expansion of the friendship pact made in August 1971 between India and the Soviet Union. Soviet interest in strategic positioning in the Indian Ocean, competitive relationship for consolidation of connections between Iran and Pakistan under the indirect influence of the United States and China, which have set themselves against the Soviet drive toward the Indian Ocean. Chinese fear of being surrounded.

18. *European Economic Community – China:* Chinese interest in a steady expansion of the EEC and in a strengthening of political cooperation between the Western European countries; as yet no general EEC policy on China.

19. *Japan - China:* Chinese fear of close ties between Japan and the USSR; reestablishment of old trade connections between China and Japan; Chinese interest in gradual break in trade connections between Japan and Taiwan. Japan most important trade partner for China today.

20. *China – oil-producing countries:* Chinese efforts to help the Arabs as counterbalance to the Soviet Union; gaining of options re: USA due to this position; expanding sphere of Africa through pro-Arab attitude in the Arab-Israeli conflict.

21. *China - India:* Continuing strained relationship; no easing of tension foreseeable in the near future.

22. *China - Pakistan:* Chinese interest in the strategic importance of Pakistan for the same reasons as the USA; communal interest between China, the USA and Pakistan relating to the Soviet-Indian friendship pact.

23. *China - East Africa:* Construction of the Uhuru railroad line from Zambia to Tanzania; China as model of a developmental policy oriented toward the emancipation of the Third World, superseding Great Britain in this region; erection of a political beachhead on the coast of East Africa. Significance of these proceedings in connection with the presence of Soviet naval units in the Indian Ocean. China's increasing importance for the African developing countries.

24. *EEC - Japan:* Good possibility for further expansion of mutual trade connections and scientific-technical cooperation. Increasing competition between Japan and the EEC in international markets; common basis for information exchange in the area of environmental protection; competitive relationship toward the Soviet Union in connection with raw material and energy problems.

25. *EEC – oil-producing countries:* Large EEC dependence on oil supply from the Middle East; no general EEC policy toward these countries; danger of individual agreements which will further weaken Western Europe's trade position; little or no pressure against the oil-producing countries.

26. *France – oil-producing countries:* Special French role in relationship to the oil-producing countries, particularly toward Iraq. French efforts to secure her own oil supplies from the Middle East and therefore to achieve a stronger position in the EEC relative to the other members. Therefore pro-Arab attitude in Arab-Israeli conflict. (Yugoslavia is in a similar position: the more independent of the USSR and the West Tito wishes to be, the more pro-Arab he must appear, in order not to be cut off from his oil supply.)

27. *France - Africa:* French efforts to expand her connections with West Africa; increasing difficulties following cultural reactions against France in the West African countries; continuing strong bilateral economic connections, particularly in the area of developmental aid.

28. *Japan - Southeast Asia:* Rapidly increasing dependence in Southeast Asia upon Japanese export economy—i.e., rising imports from Japan and concurrent reduction in Japan's dependence on shipments from Southeast Asia; possible political reaction in Southeast Asia against the increasing economic dominance of Japan.

29. *Pakistan - India:* Gradual relaxation of tension; dependence upon connections to China, the USSR and the USA for further development in this area.

The complexity of the network of connections between these countries and regions is clear even from such sketchy indications. In reality there are many more connections to take into consideration, especially when one includes the three- and four-sided coalitions. The basic characteristics of this system are as follows: (1) It is in a constant and dynamic state of flux; and (2) the gravitational fields of power are concentrated in the Northern Hemisphere, which implies that the industrial core group, in contrast to the Third World countries, maintains a self-generating dynamic. This group can therefore afford to set its policy in relation to the developing countries according to its own interests. This would strengthen the developing countries' relegation to the periphery.

Despite the widely held belief that the industrial nations are dependent upon the developing countries—due to the raw material supply, for example—it should be clear from our brief examination of the question that such a dependency does not exist. The importance of the North-South connections lies, if at all, not in the economic but in the strategic realm. Everyone is aware, however, that with the development of modern nuclear strategy it has long since become unnecessary to pursue the old policy of footholds. The importance of geographical regions has thus been reduced to their function as channels and thoroughfares for naval fleets.

If one wishes to assess the causes and consequences of growth limitation realistically, one cannot fail to see the overwhelming importance of power politics, especially since we are concerned with the limitations of only certain components of technical activities. There are, therefore, options open at a high technological level which will be decided upon in the core group's force fields of power politics, not by the developing countries.

NOTES

1. See, among others, Charles A. McClelland, *Theory and the International System* (London: The Macmillan Co., 1966); Nigel Forward, *The Field of Nations* (London: Macmillan Co., 1971), and David Vital, *The Inequality of States* (Oxford: Claredon Press, 1967).

2. See e.g.,Herbert J. Spiro, "Interdependence: A Third Option Between National Sovereignity and Supra-National Integration"(Paper presented at the IXth World Congress of the International Political Science Association, Montreal, 1973).

3. See OECD, *Science, Growth and Society. A New Perspective* (Paris 1971).

4. One of the newest representations and analysis of this issue is available in the 2nd edition of my book *Die Vierte Welt*, dtv no. 929 (Munich 1973).

5. See H. Sautter, "Regionalisierungstendenzen im Welthandel zwischen 1938 und 1970"(Paper presented at the Symposium of the Society for Economic and Social Sciences and the Institute of World Economy, Kiel, Germany, July 1973).

6. *H.-J. Rummert*, "Entwicklung des Devisenbedarfs für Energieimporte der westlichen Welt und Japans bis 1985—Konsequenzen der Anhäufung von Devisenreserven bei den Oelförderländern" (Mimeograph July 1973).

7. Ibid.

Chapter Three

The Political Consequences of the Ecological Crisis

LIMITS TO WHICH GROWTH?

Seldom do opinions clash as violently as they do in the controversy over economic growth. The ecologists say that if we do not bring the economy's exponential growth under control soon, we will be caught in a global catastrophe. This will inevitably result because our environment is being totally destroyed by the poisons being poured into it, and, at the same time, we are exhausting our reserves of raw materials. Many economists hold an opposing view: a growing economy is exactly what is needed to solve the environmental problems and to overcome possible shortages of resources through recycling and the development of new kinds of raw materials. Who is correct? Are the extremists on the economists' side who, like Wilfred Beckerman, proclaim: "As regards water pollution, for example, we are only interested in mankind, not fishkind."[1] Or are the ecologists who, along with the more responsible economists, never tires of pointing out that our present economic growth verges on ruinous exploitation and may become a burden to future generations?

From the available information, we would like to present a balanced picture out of the plethora of contradictory opinions and contentions and to show the most important relationships between economic growth and the stability of the ecosphere. This attempt will have little to do with the methodological and scientific objections raised against the MIT study by J.W. Forrester* (*World Dynamics*) and the Club of Rome's report on the limits to growth written by Dennis L. Meadows. We are much more interested in exploring three aspects of the controversy over growth limitations,

*Jay W. Forrester, *World Dynamics*, Cambridge, Mass.: Wright-Allen Press, 1971.

especially in the economic realm, which were considered too superficially in the studies mentioned above. These aspects include the *structural properties* of economic growth, the problem of *heat pollution* resulting from the use of primary energy and the *political causes and effects* as they relate to the entire growth problem.

The only economic processes relevant to environmental pollution and the problem of scarcity of resources are those directly or indirectly connected with the restructuring of matter. Certain economic areas—such as services—which are expanding both absolutely and relatively, are, with the exception of transportation, less closely or not at all tied to the restructuring of matter. Cultural achievements, most of the educational realm, the supply of problem solving techniques—in short, everything known as "software"—fits into this category. In the last analysis, mental input also remains rooted in the material metabolic cycle, but the effects of this input on the environment are so slight that we can ignore this factor. As long as these energetically irrelevant activities, which in no way pollute the environment, enter the calculation of the national income as a positive factor, this realm, roughly corresponding to the so-called "tertiary sector," will *not* have to limit its growth for environmental reasons. One must not overlook the fact, however, that the supply of nonmaterial goods within the total economic picture is closely related to both the primary (agricultural) and the secondary (industrial) sectors, because many services are necessary or even feasible only after the achievement of a certain level of economic activity. Let us consider, for example, the highly specialized services offered in patent law or in the design of a computer program.

The term "limits to growth" can therefore be applied meaningfully only to activities which necessitate additional consumption of energy. It is this region of activity which causes a great deal of dispute among certain economists and the community of ecologists, all seeking to establish the appropriate limits to growth.

The unique character of a large class of economic models stems from the fact that, proceeding from their basic premises, they describe self-adaptive processes directed toward specific equilibria. If a material becomes scarce, its price will rise relative to the prices of other goods; sales of this material will thus fall off—i.e., it will be less in demand. The producers, however, will want to take advantage of the price increase and supply even more. Finally an equilibrium price will result which will equalize supply and demand. The theory of growth also developed models which establish the existence of optimal growth patterns with intricate mathematical methods and which set out the conditions necessary for, for example, a "golden age" growth. In this model world, the concept of nonrenewable resources simply does not exist. From this perspective, environmental pollution merely signifies that *the wrong things are in the wrong place at the wrong time.* According to this view, the situation can be corrected by an economic policy which ensures that, in accordance with the pay as you pollute principle, the people responsible pay the economic costs. This would optimally synchronize the production processes with the environmental requirements and would, at the same time, foster environmental technology. New materials could be substituted for any nonrenewable resources. This view places no limits on man's ingenuity, which is why technical advancement and the accompanying economic growth are both, in theory, "limitless." This summarizes the thesis of at least some economists closely associated with the neoclassic school.

Such a conception presupposes that it would be possible, with the help of an environmentally oriented economic policy and an advanced environmental technology, to organize every process of economic transformation in a material realm, so that they all remain below the ecosystem's critical limit, even if growth continues. If one proceeds on the assumption that the global ecological cycle, which is composed of many interlocking subsystems, has a limited capacity to absorb disturbances, then "growth" would be possible only in the sense of a "growing capacity" to utilize a scarce commodity in the best possible manner. We could also formulate the problem as part of an optimalization process which maximizes material output at minimal cost, taking into consideration all the restrictions stemming from the environment's limited capacity to absorb disturbance. Using this method, one could derive an economy of a "higher order" and demonstrate that "growth," at least in the sense of "intensive growth," is compatible with the stability of the global ecosystem.

Such a possibility would be theoretically conceivable; in practical terms it is extremely unlikely, for the following reasons:

First of all, the "restrictions" on economic growth which will be consistent with the stability of the global system cannot be exactly or fully identified; a stability oriented global policy therefore could not itself be defined, even if we were optimistic enough to suppose that its realization would not encounter hostile interest groups. All that we can accomplish today is basically limited to establishing the *maximum amount of various toxic materials* allowed to enter the environment. This measure will hardly be sufficient to fit all the material turnover processes of human activity into the closed cycle of the biosphere; it is only a first and probably inadequate step. That is to say, it is entirely possible that even in a zero discharge production technology, the earth's complicated ecosystem could still become trapped in a critical instability.

We now come to the problem of heat pollution. When people discuss economic growth, they usually refer to so-called exponential growth. This is a form of growth whose *relative* rate of increase over a period of time remains constant. This type of increase corresponds to the concept of compound interest. Every exponential growth is characterized by the fact that it very quickly develops astronomical proportions. If, for example, the national income grows six percent per year, it will take only 28 years for it to quintuple, and in 40 years the national income will have risen to ten times its original level.

Limits will therefore occur sooner or later during the exponential growth process of an economy due to:

the exhaustion of nonrenewable natural resources,
the overburdening of the environment with toxic materials and
    equilibrium-disturbing processes, and
food scarcity in the case of a continually growing population.

An *expansion of the space for growth* can be achieved

in the area of resources, through recycling and substitution;
in the area of environmental pollution, through technical measures
    for environmental protection; and
in the area of food production, through new methods of production,
    including synthetic foods and new ways of generating protein.

Let us be optimistic and suppose that the restructuring of the production process has reached the zero discharge level. Let us further suppose that the problem of raw materials has been solved with recycling, substitution and the discovery of many new reserves and that the rehabilitation of the environment has been achieved with environmentally considerate technology. Have we therefore produced the famous "spaceship economy," and will we now be able to live in eternal harmony with our environment? The answer depends upon whether the energy consumption necessary to maintain these ideal conditions, and whether the vast heat inevitably connected with this energy, will disturb the natural equilibrium of the flow of solar radiation in and out of the earth atmosphere system. Let us give some orders of magnitude [2]: the total amount of solar radiation directed at the earth measures 10^{14} kw. The earth atmosphere system gives off, except for a very small share of the energy which is connected with photosynthesis, almost exactly the same amount.

Thirty-five percent is directly reflected back into space, 22 percent is absorbed by the atmosphere and given off again, and 43 percent reaches the earth's surface and is transformed into heat. The problem is that the natural equilibrium flow of solar radiation in and out of the earth atmosphere system can be easily disturbed by the use of primary energy connected with economic activity (the restructuring of matter). The possibility of disturbances is made more likely by the fact that an expansion of environmentally consistent space for growth using environmental protection measures and recycling, and assuming there is a growing population, the increase in agricultural production and/or productivity, will require more energy.

In 1970, world use of *primary energy* stood at 55.10^{12} kwh per year. That corresponds to approximately 1/220 percent of the mean solar energy supply. The question arises as to when the earth's use of primary energy will reach 1 percent or 10 percent of the average supply of solar energy. If one accepts the UN estimate, which predicts an average growth rate in world energy use of 5.7 percent up to the year 2000, and one assumes, very optimistically, that this rate of growth will not increase, then the 1 percent figure would be reached in *95 years*. It will take 75 years for the continents alone to use 1 percent of the solar energy supply. By analogy, the following values hold, using 1970 as the starting point: for the USA—60 years; for West Germany—7 years. If one calculates how long it will take for the amount of primary energy necessary for human activities to reach 10 percent of the average solar energy supply, the following statistics result*:

Earth surface: 140 years (at a 5.7 percent growth rate per year)
Continents: 115 years (at a 5.7 percent growth rate per year)
USA: 120 years (at a 4.0 percent growth rate per year)
Northeast USA: 80 years (at a 4.0 percent growth rate per year)
West Germany: 67 years (at a 4.0 percent growth rate per year)

At our present level of knowledge, it is estimated that an increase of 1 percent in the energy supplied to the earth atmosphere system will result in a temperature change of from 1 to 1.5° C (approximately 1.4 to 2.7° F). With the present rate of increase in the consumption of primary energy we must therefore face the fact that in 150 years, at the latest, the *equilibrium flow of the "solar radiation– earth atmosphere" system will be critically disturbed.* The specific

*K.M. Meyer-Abich, Die ökologische Grenze des Wirtschaftswachstums in Rundschau No. 72, (1972) Heft 20.

consequences of the climate changes in the earth atmosphere system brought on by the warming trend cannot yet be predicted. If one considers, however, that a global temperature change of only a few degrees centigrade would make the difference between an ice age and our present climatic situation, one can gather that in the very near future, historically speaking, the world climate will be deeply and perhaps irreversibly changed by these processes.

We maintain, therefore, that a production structure consistent with the environment's carrying capacity is a necessary but not a sufficient condition for the maintenance of our ecosystem's global equilibrium. More importantly, the assimilation of a modern technical society's material productive processes within the general circulation of matter within the environment must be achieved with a level of energy consumption which will *not* disturb the equilibrium between solar radiation–earth atmosphere. No one has yet calculated precisely whether or not it is still possible to stay beneath this crucial limit, given the level of material production. The dilemma results from the fact that we must reduce our energy consumption in the long run, but in the future we will need *more energy* for technical environmental protection projects and recycling.

Is there a way out of this dilemma? One could try to expand the *utilization of solar energy*, since this form of energy consumption causes no disturbance in the thermodynamic equilibrium. Even with the swiftest technical advances in the development of solar cells, however, this mode of energy utilization is severely limited. The options remaining include the utilization of water power, geothermal resources or tidal energy. In relation to expected global energy needs, these energy sources are either insufficient or not completely usable. If, on the other hand, one adds to the fossil fuel the energy stores potentially available in nuclear materials, one could consider the world's total energy supply as a practically limitless one. It is the waste heat resulting from the utilization of these energy sources which sets limits on our energy consumption, and it is these limits which then constrain the permissible activity levels in the remainder of man's conversions of matter, including the economic ones.

It would not be surprising if the first rough estimate of these "permissible activity levels" led to the discovery that today's industrial countries have already "overshot" the permissible world standard. Because there are also countries whose material activity levels measure one-fortieth of America's, the solution to the problem would involve an international redistribution of activity levels on the basis of a quota system. Complicating the situation is the fact that, through the utilization of the fossil and nuclear energies stored in the earth, we will be raising the system's entropy and thereby the degree of its instability.[3]

Actually, there should be no material antagonism between economy and ecology. If any arose during the development of economics as science, it happened because the economists specialized in the analysis of a subsystem whose regulative mechanisms are limited to the interaction of special (convex) production and utility functions and assumed the existence of free goods. From this relatively narrow base, with much intellectual effort, economic theory created a closed and consistent world. This world compiled findings— especially in the area of growth theory—that sometimes are able to inspire mathematicians. These findings are unfortunately only of purely intellectual interest and are totally irrelevant to the solution of the real growth problems which we see facing us today.

Let us summarize our findings up to now: the problem of the *limits to growth* exists only in connection with those activities which deal with the restructuring of matter. Limitations can result through *overburdening the environment* with pollutants, through a *shortage of raw materials*, through the *contraction of food production areas* as the population expands, as well as through direct influx of *heat from energy* consumption.

Certain irrelevant activities in terms of energy use—such as services—are calculated into the GNP, but there exist no direct limitations to growth for this area of economic activity; therefore the GNP can still grow. There is, however, an indirect limitation, to the extent that the demand for and the availability of services are related to the level of material restructuring in the other sectors of the economy.

If it were possible to perfect technical environmental protection using an omnipotent environmental technology to the point where all processes were at a zero discharge level and to solve the problem of raw materials through continuous recycling and substitution, and even if we were also in the position to expand the space for food production using an environmentally consistent production increase of both natural and synthetic foods, we could still not guarantee ourselves the ideal equilibrium state within the ecosystem. We could only hope for true stability if it were possible to achieve a state of zero discharge with rising total production, increasing recycling and self-expanding space for food production using energy inputs whose level in relation to accumulation of waste heat would not disturb the equilibrium flow between solar radiation—earth atmosphere. It remains to be seen whether, with today's technologies, this state is at all achievable at a level of material transformation sufficient for the human race as a whole, or whether a worldwide redistribution of energy-relevant activity levels must take place between developed industrial nations and the developing countries.

We now come to the political aspect of growth limitation. The international redistribution of activity levels is only one side of the problem. The other side results from the limited performance of the market system. Theoretically speaking, there is an equilibrium price for every level of scarcity; that is, a price level exists where the demand is exactly as large as the supply. In reality, however, the price of a certain commodity cannot rise indefinitely, because at a certain level problems of social justice enter the picture. If, for example, the price of gasoline rises to $8 a gallon, the question will arise as to whether this price is as fair to a midwife who must drive to remote villages in the country as it is to the rich playboy who takes his girlfriends for drives in his Jaguar. The same principle comes up in connection with food rationing during a war. Because every rationing must follow criteria which take into consideration factors other than purchasing power, we end up with the political problem of assessment and choice of criteria. One can assume that the regulatory capacity of the Western industrial nations' market mechanism, which is corrected by taxes and subsidies, is not yet totally exhausted; after a certain point, however, we will very clearly have to make political decisions. This trend is, in part, already in effect today. Standards for tolerance levels, principles of space allocation, models for new towns are all examples of areas necessitating political decisions. In contrast to wartime food rationing, the selection, the specification and the evaluation of criteria are much more difficult for an ecologically oriented restructuring of the growth process. The restructuring must be based upon exact data from different scientific specialists as well as on the possible technical solutions offered by the engineers—all difficult problems, especially in view of the uncertainty of many of the measurements and estimates of ecological interrelations. Such uncertainties lead to stalemates in the political sphere, since no party is prepared to take on the responsibility as long as it cannot be clearly proven that, for example, one particular party has caused environmental damage and must therefore bear the costs of damages and prevention.

In general, however, the developed industrial nations are, due to their more advanced technical skills, in a much better position to cope with these problems than the developing countries where, although they exist on a lower level of economic activity, the problems are no less complex.[4] In one respect, however, the developing countries are ahead of us, at least temporarily. They are still living in the realm of basic needs and have not yet been caught up in the process of the production of artificial needs or the consumer drive. They could therefore achieve a pattern of economic growth which conforms to the environment and at the same time improves the standard of living through the use of products systematically built to last longer. It is here and not in the new and growing environmental protection industries where the real chance lies for a resolution to the contradiction between growth limitation and the maintenance—or improvement—of the material standard of living, a contradiction which until now had seemed an insurmountable obstacle.[5]

In the long run, the world must discover a dynamic equilibrium between man's technical-economic activities and their effects on the environment. That would be possible, without a reduction in our standard of living, only if we could succeed in immediately halting the population growth. That is flatly impossible. The world population could be stabilized at seven to nine billion by the year 2010, however. Until then we will have to deal both with the rising aspirations of today's 3.9 billion humans and the material needs of the coming four to five billion people. This will cause an international run on raw materials as well as on additional capital expenditures for research and new technology for environmental protection, raw material substitution, recycling and the expansion of new energy sources. The situation will be aggravated by the necessity to eliminate the environmental disturbances we have already set in motion. Due to all of these factors, the real standard of living in the next years will either sink or at least not grow as rapidly as it has up to now.

That will once again lead, both domestically and on an international level, to an intensified struggle over distribution and therefore to social unrest—in other words, to an intensification of the international class struggle.

It is these political and social problems which, during the process of growth limitation, are already overwhelming us, long before we reach the absolute, fixed limits of growth, a situation which would arise due to the waste heat from our energy consumption, even if we were in the position to increase material production without burdening the environment.

ECOLOGY AND INTERNATIONAL POLITICS

One hears much discussion today concerning the exhaustion of the reserves of raw materials and energy sources. Before these possibilities cause difficulties, however, we will be faced with much more serious problems due to the increasing shortage of a basically more important "resource"—*the carrying capacity of the biosphere.* The capacity, according to all we understand today about the many interlocking feedback processes, is limited. The conflict between the industrial countries and the developing countries will prove to be a redistribution struggle over the relative shares of this theoretically constant environmental carrying capacity. H. Rausch described the situation very astutely:

> Today's environmental pollution derives, for the most part, from that third of mankind which lives in the industrialized countries; if the other two-thirds were to duplicate the process of industrialization, global pollution would, due to this fact alone, and totally disregarding the continuing growth of the industrial nations, increase to some multiple of today's proportions; the problem therefore lies in how to steer the development in the Third World so that it places as little burden as possible on the environment.[6]

Figure 3–1 illustrates this state of affairs.

Presently, the largest share of environmental pollution is caused by the industrial countries; this is shown by curve (1). Due to their economic growth, the developing countries are now also polluting the environment, although on a much lower scale; this is illustrated by curve (2). Beginning with the present situation, signified by a vertical line, we see that the total environmental pollution level deriv-

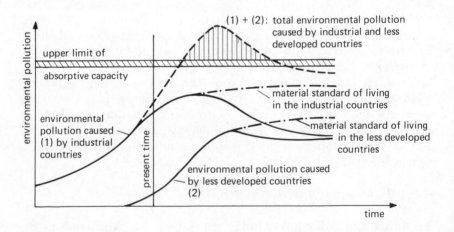

Figure 3–1.

ing from the sum of both groups' contribution (dotted line), still lies beneath the maximum pollution limit. Even if we very optimistically assume that it will shortly be possible for the industrial countries to reduce environmental pollution both relatively and absolutely, the probability that we will overshoot the maximum level of pollution is still very large, because of the fact that in the meantime economic growth, and the pollution accompanying it, will be stepped up in the developing countries. Let us again be optimistic and assume that these countries will eventually be both willing and in a position to reduce their pollutant level both relatively and absolutely. The pollution levels of both groups would then be about equal. One could conceive that we could thus very possibly come through the critical phase unscathed.

Even if we base all of our considerations on these optimistic assumptions, however, we will not be able to avoid an overload on the environment. The material standard of living of the industrial and developing countries will—and this is once again optimistic—not rise, but reach a certain equilibrium level at which a difference will still remain between the level of the industrial countries and that of the developing countries. One could very easily derive a much less encouraging and perhaps more realistic picture from these givens. According to Forrester and Meadows, overshooting the limit to the biosphere's carrying capacity is inextricably connected with a drastic reduction in the material standard of living. This would imply that we would have to expect an absolute reduction, not merely an adjustment, at a certain level. It is obvious what the consequences, in terms of a global conflict situation, will be.

How should we assess such a presentation, and what are the chances that the international ecological policy will be able to escape the destiny outlined here? Before we can thoroughly answer these questions, we must examine the meaning of "the burden on the biosphere" more closely. It is in this connection that I came upon a formulation of Professor J. M. Burgers, which goes back to 1943 (!):

> The overwhelming majority of human dealings consist in the construction of patterns of order at the cost of something which from another perspective is a pattern in itself. A more precise awareness of this phenomenon is of great practical significance, especially in connection with the fact that (aside from the solar energy) the earth is a closed milieu for us. The thoughtless destruction and especially the negligent dumping of scrap and waste products with no consideration of the consequences will bring on the threat of impoverishment and poisoning, the gravity of which we can hardly comprehend.

Professor Burgers then continues:

> As long as the number of humans was smaller, this question was of limited importance, because new regions could always be utilized in place of the ones which had been ruined, and meanwhile regenerative forces were at work in the natural surroundings. Now, however, the areas of this activity cover practically the entire earth, which fact has become clearer to us now than ever before.[7]

One might guess that these quotations were taken from one of the many publications which concern themselves today with the problem of environmental protection. Historically speaking, there have always been disturbances in the biosphere. They can occur from natural causes—i.e., volcanic eruptions or earthquakes—or be caused by humans (the so-called anthropogenic cause). During the earth's historical development, global climate changes occurred which have not yet been fully explained. We know that after the appearance of higher forms of life on the earth—that is, 550 million years ago—the atmosphere's oxygen content rose by from one to two powers of ten. Both poles were free of ice during 90 percent of this time, while widespread inland ice domes built up four to six times during the last millions of years in North America and Europe.[8] The biosphere is characterized by an almost infinite number of interlocking feedbacks and dynamic equilibria which in the course of millions of years have achieved the present degree of complexity and relative stability. The following traits characterize this complex system: it is, first of all, highly organized; further, it came into existence, as has already been indicated, during different geological epochs; and, finally, it has the autogenic ability to reestablish its own equilibrium within certain bounds. If these bounds are overstepped, a complete collapse results, similar to the phenomenon of "dying" lakes which we can observe today. Human effects on the biosphere can be typified as follows: (1) by the high level of activity, and therefore by a now even more significant influence on the global processes within the biosphere; and (2) by the economic-technical process' inherent tendency to accelerate.

If one compares these two phenomena—namely, the characteristics of the biosphere on the one hand, and those of human activity on the other—it becomes clear that at least two massive obstacles stand in the way of a policy keyed to the protection of the biosphere. First of all, we do not have very much time at our disposal as long as the anthropogenic activities continue to increase at an exponential rate. Second, we know much too little about the complex interactions between man and the biosphere to be able to derive any detailed guidelines for our practical behavior. Due to this situation, it is then conceivable that the urgently needed practical measures will be delayed or even totally blocked.

We have already pointed out that the globalism of the ecological effects clashes with the sovereignty of the states. In reality this conflict goes even farther, since not only nations but also households, towns, regions and—going beyond the nations—international organizations are involved. A conflict of interest can sometimes occur within these individual groups, as it does, for example, on an international plane between the industrial and the developing countries. The conflict was made very clear at the conference in Stockholm on environmental protection. There the developing countries maintained that they too had environmental problems—namely, poverty, lack of housing, malnutrition, contaminated water and lack of medical care. On the basis of immediate living conditions, the environment is much more threatening to the people in the developing countries than to those in the industrial countries. This conference therefore demanded that the industrial states refrain from initiating any new trade restrictions affecting the developing countries under the pretext of environmental protection and that the measures for environmental protection not proceed at the expense of foreign aid.

The relationship of the developing countries to the industrial countries is determined, in the long run, by two factors which are the subject matter of ongoing investigations: (1) by the effects of a shortage of raw materials, and (2) by the effects of technology on the economic and societal situation of the developing countries. The World Bank examined the question of to what extent in the immediate future the developing countries will be in the position—similar to the oil countries—to carry through OPECs blackmail strategy in certain raw material sectors against the industrial countries. It has been established that large reserves of scarce raw materials such as copper and tin lie in the developing countries, while other raw materials are all found either in the developed Western industrial nations or in the socialistic economies. The distribution given by the World Bank looks like the representation given in Table 3–1.

These findings do not eliminate the possiblity that the developing countries will be able to profit from general price increases in raw materials during the next few years. These increases will probably remain within limits, however, since even with increased resource consumption at a growth rate of 4 to 5 percent per year, reserves of most raw materials will still exist. According to the World Bank's calculations of the present and future consumption increases, these reserves will suffice 1,700 years for potash, 350 years for chromium and 100 years for iron. Today's known reserves of sulfur, bauxite,

Table 3-1. Reserves of Selected Minerals (regional distribution in percent)

	Industrial countries	Developing countries	Socialistic countries
Copper	37	47	16
Tungsten	13	12	75
Lead	66	21	13
Zinc	65	23	12
Tin	4	79	17
Silver	40	24	36

Source: International Bank for Reconstruction and Development, "What are the opportunities for raising LDS's earnings from exports of nonfuel minerals through OPEC-type cooperation?" Memorandum, 1972.

cobalt, nickel, manganese, molybdenum and titanium should last approximately 50 to 70 years.

In summary, then, one can say that blackmail as we experienced it from the oil sector is highly unlikely during the next ten to 20 years. The fact is that the relatively few scarce raw materials—i.e., copper and tin—with deposits in the developing countries lie in countries which are too weak to pursue an extortionist policy.

The weight given to the other aspect—namely, the role of technical advancement—varies. While the group of experts who prepared the so-called Founex report for the Stockholm conference attach great significance to the positive effects of technical advancement, the Japanese group in Stockholm, referring to their own experience, expressed some skepticism. After a closer examination of the interrelationships one must also tend toward skepticism. Technology transfer, as we all know, takes place to a great extent through multinational corporations. We are dealing with technologies, however, which are adapted to the needs of the multinational corporations and not necessarily to the needs of the developing countries. Beyond this fact, these multinational firms can still operate virtually unregulated. They therefore play a very ambivalent role in the whole process. They are no longer regulated by the nation states and they have not yet come under the control of the developing countries. In this position they have a large margin of freedom, of which they take advantage to strengthen their own economic positions.

We have recognized that every developmental process must at bottom involve ecological repercussions because by definition it establishes a new order in place of the old one and thereby, to the extent that this new order involves metabolic cycles, disturbs the natural cycles existing up to that point. Technical-economic advancement

can therefore very easily go hand in hand with ecological catastrophe. Through communication with these developing countries we
transfer our Western values—including technology—and thereby
destroy the societal and natural equilibria which have developed
there over hundreds of years. This process has long since been set
into motion and can no longer be reversed. For these reasons, the
international community stands, for the first time in its history,
before the necessity of executing a global ecological policy. The
community is trapped by the demands, which the West stimulated
and which have now been intensified by the developing countries.
The turn of events since the conference in Stockholm does not look
promising. A secretariat was set up in Nairobi and a fund of $100
million was set up that is supposed to suffice for the first five years'
expenses. That amount is 1/10,000 of what is spent annually for
defense. It is better than nothing, but, measured against the dimensions of the expenditures which will be necessary, it is woefully
inadequate. We can therefore assume that the developing countries,
under the impression that it will be impossible to attain a material
standard of living comparable to the industrial nations', will grasp at
measures which will force the industrial nations to use the technology they have developed in the process of polluting the environment as a weapon against the developing countries.

One must nevertheless applaud the efforts toward global environmental protection made up to now, modest as they have been. These
include the programs of the EEC, the efforts of the Council of
Europe, the activities of the OECD and the experiences acquired up
to now within the realm of the GATT. Morris Strong, director of the
UN Environmental Secretariat in Nairobi, wrote a very interesting
treatise on the UN's future responsibilities in the area of environmental protection. He envisages a future organizational system in
which the different specialized organizations, including the nongovernmental ones, will unite on the basis of broad public support to
form a network in which information will be available and, more
importantly, a political unity will be created which should take the
place of the UN's nonexistent executive and therefore realize a global
ecological policy which will serve every member of the world. In
view of the fundamental economic conflicts which dominate today,
however, it seems highly unlikely that this kind of policy will be able
to create a "world cartel renouncing growth."* Such a cartel or even
an international nonproliferation treaty in the area of economic

*G. Bombach, Planspiele Zum Überleben, in: Mitteilungen der List Gessel-
schaft, Fasc. 8, Nr. 1, 1973.

growth would provide the necessary conditions for the avoidance of any overburdening of the ecological system such as that illustrated in Figure 3–1 by the cross-hatched area.

THE INTERACTION OF SUBSYSTEMS

In the course of the last 8,000 years, man has, on the one hand, converted approximately 11 percent of the available land surface to agricultural use; another 20 percent serves as pasture land.[10] On the other hand, in his industrial agglomerations man is also destroying his own living space with exhaust fumes, noise, filth, etc. at a rate that within just a few years produced a complete change in his attitudes, for example, toward the automobile. It has also become clear that the interaction between man and the biosphere extends over a very broad and highly differentiated area, in terms of both time and space. It has taken only a few years to make the transition from the more or less indifferent acceptance of exhaust fumes, stinking water, etc. as an inevitable by-product of technical-economic advancement to the vehement refusal, for example, to construct new atomic energy plants. In this era—infinitesimal compared to man's 8,000 year old agricultural history—contemporary modes of behavior, norms and values have fundamentally changed under the influence of practical experiences. This means that in addition to the technical-physical, economic and institutional factors we must also deal with norms and values which are on the one hand determined by physical, ecological, technical, economic and institutional factors, but which on the other hand influence these factors through many feedbacks. One can create a reliable picture of the complexity of the network between man and the biosphere only if one examines these components as strata in a differentiated world model. In the study *Limits to Growth*, the Club of Rome took the first step toward this type of integrated analysis of the interconnections, using system dynamics. Certain important elements—for example, the political and the institutional strata—were not included in the analysis, however.

The eight strata world model developed by Mesarovic and Pestel shows great promise in showing the complex interconnections (see Figure 3–2).[11]

The geophysical stratum forming the models' base includes environmental phenomena within geophysical time scales—that is, processes which take place in 10^4 to 10^9 years. The ecological stratum primarily relates to phenomena in the biosphere. The time scale for these occurrences ranges from a few years to a few thousand years. The technological stratum covers the energy-relevant processes of

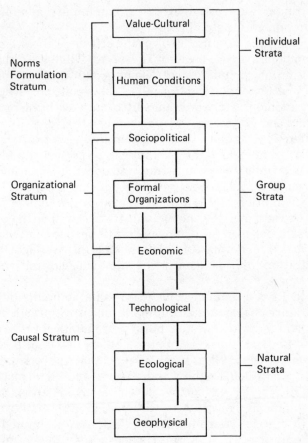

Source: M.D. Mesarovic and E.C. Pestel. A goal-seeking and Regionalized Model for Analysis of Critical World Relationships. The Conceptual Foundation, in: Kybernetes, 1972. Vol. 1, p. 84.

Figure 3-2.

material transformation that man undertakes with technological aid and energy consumption. The economic stratum includes all economically relevant processes: not everything that is technically feasible is economically useful. This stratum basically covers all allocations of human activity which relate to a maximizing of certain objective functions under restrictive conditions—the core of the economic problem.

The "formal organizations" stratum involves the functions of "those societal groupings which have specific goals and corresponding infrastructure, for example, firms, community administrations, government apparatus, etc."[12]

The sociopolitical stratum involves the effects of the interaction of families, political parties, civil initiatives, etc. While the "human conditions" stratum includes man's living conditions, taking health, nutrition, etc. into consideration, the "value-cultural" stratum contains every moment which we generally occupy with the problems of values, ethics and norms.

The different strata have been further grouped at different levels. The natural strata include the geophysical, ecological and technological substrata, while the group strata include the economic, formal organizations and sociopolitical phenomena and the individual strata the human condition and value-cultural categories. At the same time the causal stratum includes the natural strata as well as the economic, the organizational stratum extends from the economic to the sociopolitical, and the norms formulation stratum overlaps the sociopolitical stratum while encompassing the value-cultural and human condition strata.

This model has a significant heuristic value. It points out connections and derives categories according to cognitive principles, on the one hand, and indicates the possibilities for empirical verification, on the other. Beyond these attributes, the model is also anthropocentric—that is, centered around man—so that the orientation and values exist according to the standards and requirements of man's existence. The model was further developed by Mesarović and Pestel and was empirically constructed, with special attention given to the economic submodel. Hartmut Bossel [13] has attempted both to express the processes of norm change within the norm stratum empirically and to adapt them to a computer simulation process. The work includes the listing of relevant norms and delineating the processes of norm change, as well as connecting the norm stratum with its surroundings and with the causal decision strata of the Mesarovic-Pestel system. Norm structures have already been simulated and the influence of norm hierarchies on the behavior of the whole system has been investigated.

As I have already indicated, Forrester's "Systems Dynamics" method forms the basis for the Forrester-Meadows model. This method allows a quick and graphic representation of complex connections, but it is mechanical and deterministic. All structural parameters are fixed, so that computer runs can be influenced only by a change in the parameters or the initial conditions. This method therefore does not permit the consideration of sociological, political or psychological factors.

Mesarovic and Pestel have attempted to develop a computer-oriented planning and decision model which allows the effects of alternative measures and strategies to be judged, taking the conventional as well as political and psychological factors into consideration. This model's basic characteristics including the following:

1. The world system will be represented by a number of connecting, mutually influencing regions. The model presently operates with ten such regions. The countries included in any one region should be comparable in relation to their problems and their economic developments.
2. The decisionmaking and goal-finding processes which are influential in the long term development are explicitly represented on the regional level. This makes it possible to examine and represent human society as an adaptive system.
3. The Mesarovic-Pestel model is based on the theory of the hierarchical multistrata system. It allows the integration of our knowledge and data from any problem area through the categorization into strata and substrata.
4. The model is not deterministic and is therefore fundamentally different from Forrester's.

This model has been developed sufficiently to allow actual simulation runs. The economic submodel was refined and further expanded a few months ago. The model of regional population growth also belongs with this group; it helped to analyze the effects of different birth control programs in individual regions. A submodel for world energy supply, including a decisionmaking model which applies alternative strategies to the energy crisis is also in existence. Further submodels are being developed—a model for food production and the world's phosphorus supply, as well as an energy model and a model for the technological and the ecological strata.

It is obvious that two model builders cannot implement such a vast program alone. From the beginning Mesarovic and Pestel were fully aware that the expansion and structuring of their submodels would depend upon the exchange of ideas with qualified specialists. In this way, further expansion and improvement of the economic submodel occurred in close cooperation with a group of particularly interested economists. Since then Mesarovic and Pestel have published several reports on this "multilevel world model."[14]

I have pointed out that this attempt is of great heuristic value. It can be further utilized as a systematically applied search and learn process particularly appropriate to the generation of scenarios of possible world conditions with their peculiar attributes. Such scenarios permit us to identify every indicator which is strategically important for the maintenance of the total system's functioning capacity and thereby for man's chances for survival within this system.

The recognition process vital for human survival requires the creation of these hierarchical multilevel systems and the explicit simulation of scenarios so that strategic indicators can be identified and so that the model can function in a practical manner. This will not be a linear process running merrily along its track; it will be a step-by-step expansion of our perceptive horizons using a computer-oriented dialogue as a replica of complex reality. Association with such systems has made one point clear; there is a difference between physical and biological systems. In comparison to biological systems, physical systems are simple. They have a relatively low degree of dimensionality; they are, unlike biological systems, linear; and, above all, they are invariant with time, whereas the structure of biological systems changes as a function of time (evolution). Physical systems are either deterministic or stochastic, while biological systems are adaptive and goalseeking, which better suits the analysis of evolutionary processes.

The relationships of the subsystems within a technical system are clearly defined and fixed, while the biological subsystems are, as a result of the time variation, changeable. Finally, technical systems are not, as a rule, redundant, while redundancies abound in biological systems.

Social systems are a mixture of technical and biological systems. From this perspective, the Mesarovic-Pestel system includes elements from physical-technical, biological and social systems. Although it is hierarchically constructed, with its complexity and goal-seeking character, it comes very close to being a biological system.[15]

We are only at the beginning of our dialogue with this conception of reality. The following pages will show how productive this dialogue can be. The following problem areas emerge from the relations between Mesarovic and Pestel's eight strata:

Value-Cultural/Human Condition Strata: on the one hand the self-realization of man, on the other the change of consciousness through the concrete conditions of human existence.

Value-Cultural/Sociopolitical Strata: on the one hand participation, on the other motivation and innovation.

Value-Cultural/Formal Organizations Strata: codification of values into norms through adaptive organizational forms, development of a consistent system of norms. Seen from the organizational side: molding of values through organizations, such as churches and schools, that are suited for system-supporting norm codification.

Value-Cultural/Economic Strata: on the one hand utility functions, production of needs (not just commodities); on the other hand autonomous effect of the economic process on the system of values (consumer society, throw-away society, etc.).

Value-Cultural/Technological Strata: technology for man through technology assessment; but also influence of technology of value engineering on individuals' value structure, proliferation through news broadcast, change in aspirations and therefore time horizons.

Value-Cultural/Ecological Strata: consciousness-raising in connection with the incorporation of man into the evolutionary process; consciousness of the relationship between culture and nature and man's role in this relationship.

Value-Cultural/Geophysical Strata: setting priorities in research which correspond to human values; therefore, too, consciousness of the involved time dimensions—i.e., thermodynamic global balances.

Human Conditions/Sociopolitical Strata: feudalization, emancipation of the developing countries. Also, international structural policy aimed at achieving a more equitable income distribution both intra- and internationally.

Human Conditions/Formal Organizations Strata: formation of international organizations such as UNCTAD, FAO, IDA; on the other hand, influence of these organizations on living conditions both in the sense of furthering development and a possible hardening of existing exploitive structures.

Human Conditions/Economic Strata: capacity to save (capital formation), labor force, its contribution to GNP, etc.; on the other hand, improvement of living conditions through economic growth, particularly in the area of satisfaction of basic needs (social indicators).

Human Conditions/Technological Strata: society's capacity to absorb technical innovation; on the other hand, influence of societal living conditions by exponential processes occurring through technology—i.e., in the area of communications, operations, computers, range capacity, etc.

Human Conditions/Ecological Strata: societal ability to pursue an active environmental policy; from the other side, limitation of living conditions through consumer drives, shortage of resources, shortages of food-producing areas (limits to growth).

Human Conditions/Geophysical Strata: societal ability to systematize scientific data on geophysical conditions. From the other side: influence on living conditions by long term climatic changes, which are, in turn, triggered by human activities (restructuring materials, energy consumption, waste heat).

Sociopolitical/Formal Organizations Strata: new international organizations or new functions for existing organizations, such as the World Bank's income policy, the activities of UNESCO, etc. From the other side, influence by churches, insurance companies, the government on sociopolitical factors.

Sociopolitical/Economic Strata: equitable income distribution versus efficient allocation of production factors; also, trade-off between present high consumption with a long term smaller growth rate, as well as present sacrifice (maximal capital accumulation) to achieve a long term maximalization of growth (social discount rate).

Sociopolitical/Technology Strata: medium technology, appropriate technology in the developing countries. General: no more technology-oriented criteria for efficiency. Technology in the service of social policy: data banks, social insurance, etc.

Sociopolitical/Ecological Strata: conflict between environmental protection and distribution policy, danger of neglecting ecology due to pretended sociopolitical requirements. Therefore, on whom does the burden of environmental policy and protection devolve? A current question both nationally and internationally.

Sociopolitical/Geophysical Strata: no recognizable direct connection at present.

Formal Organization/Economic Strata: multinational cooperations, ECOSOC, World Bank, etc.; on the other side, economic political control systems, economic order.

Formal Organization/Technological Strata: support of technology through institutions such as the Institute for System Technology and Innovation Research (ISI, Karlsruhe, Germany), the Stanford Research Institute (SRI) or Battelle; governmental research support; the entire research and development system in the USA and the developed European countries. On the other hand, technology serving organizational research (see E. Jantsch's* more recent investigations).

Formal Organization/Ecological Strata: Stockholm conference, agreement re protection of the oceans, etc. On the other side: initiation of formal procedures which, for example, implement the "Pay-as-you-Pollute"-principle (now acknowledged by the OECD).

Formal Organization/Geophysical Strata: for example, geophysical year and the research organizations developed from it.

Economic/Technological Strata: research and development expenditures, technology forecasting (Jantsch, deMartino); seen in the opposite direction, change in production functions due to technical factors, influence of technical advances on economic growth.

Economic/Ecological Strata: recycling, substitution of raw materials, broadening of space for food production, reduction in population growth, etc.

Economic/Geophysical Strata: search for new resources using Skylab; financial limits; setting research priorities.

Technological/Ecological Strata: environmental technology; application of technology to control the ecosystem's instabilities; new energy sources which do not disturb the earth's thermal balance, like solar energy.

Technological/Geophysical Strata: thousands of research projects all over the world devoted to the geophysical exploration of our

*Eric Jantsch, Design of Evolution, Brazillier, New York, 1975.

environment; estimation of the "absolute limits" within which the human species can survive.

Ecological/Geophysical Strata: ecological processes are a function of fundamental geophysical laws. Man cannot change these laws; he can only adapt his behavior according to his insights into the system's connections (adjust his interference with the environment) so that his chances for survival in the evolutionary process are maximized.

I believe that this short digression reveals how productive the multilevel system is when we want to formulate what the problem areas are. As soon as we must provide solutions to problems, however, we cannot be satisfied with their verbal description of specific problems; we must make all the variations on the complex connections transparent. We therefore require the support of a computer, since no human brain and no language can complete this task alone. One should therefore consider the verbal description and the computer-supported analysis of complex systems as complementary methods, not as antagonistic processes.

In his historical development up to this point, man has learned to control the following systems:

T systems (territorial systems),
M systems (machine systems),
M-M systems (man-machine systems—i.e., the Apollo project).

The following systems are not yet under man's control:

S systems (social systems such as economic, urban, etc.)
B systems (biological systems such as cancer cells, hormonal control, etc.)
E systems (ecosystems—the interaction of social structures, technical processes, norm changes and the environment)

Like the biological systems, the E systems vary with time and can, in principle, be organized as adaptive goal-seeking systems. Man's chances for survival in fact depend upon whether these E systems will function properly in time.

NOTES

1. Wilfred Beckermann, "Economists and Environmental Catastrophe," *Oxford Economic Papers*, November 1972.

2. See K.M. Meyer-Abich, "Die ökologische Grenze des Wirtschaftswachstums," *Rundschau* 72 (1972), Heft 20. Also see M. King Hubbert, "The Energy Resources of the Earth," *Scientific American*, 224, 3 (September 1971); Hermann Flohn, "Klimaschwankung oder Klima-Modifikation?" in *Arbeiten zur Allgemeinen Klimatologie* (Darmstadt 1971), pp.291-309.

3. See Nicholas Georgescu-Roegen, *The Entropy Law and the Economic Process* Cambridge, Mass.: Harvard University Press, (1971).

4. See in addition to the highly informative study by Maurice F. Strong, "One Year after Stockholm. An Ecological Approach to Management," *Foreign Affairs* 51, 4 (July 1973): 691-707. Among other things, Strong astutely observes: "ecocatastrophes of which we hear so much are much *more* likely to occur in the poorer countries than in the wealthier ones, since the latter have the resources to deal with these problems or at least to put off their full impact" (p. 691).

5. See G. Bruckmann, "Grenzen welchen Wachstums? "(lecture manuscript Vienna 1972,); James Brian Quinn, "Next big industry: environmental improvement," *Harvard Business Review*, September-October 1971, pp. 120ff.

6. H. Rausch, "Die Dritte Welt und die Postulate des Umweltschutzes," *Neue Zürcher Zeitung*, July 23, 1972, issue no. 200.

7. J.M. Burgers, "Over de verhouding tussen het entropiebegrip en de levensfuncties," *Verhandelingen Ned. akademie van wetenschappen*, Afd. natuurkunde 1943, 1ᵉ sectie, D1. XVIII, no. 3, p. 39. Cited in: J. Huizinga, *Wenn die Waffen schweigen* (Basle 1945), p. 115.

8. See H. Flohn, "Natürliche und anthropogene Klimamodifikationen," *Annalen der Meteorologie*, Neue Folge, no. 6(1973), pp. 59-66; "Die Tätigkeit des Menschen als Klimafaktor," *Z. Erdk.* 9 (1941), pp. 13-22.

9. Strong, 690-707.

10. See Flohn, "Natürliche und anthropogene Klimamodifikationen," p. 63.

11. M.D. Mesarovic and E.C. Pestel, "A Goal-seeking and Regionalized Model for Analysis of Critical World Relationships — The Conceptual Foundation," *Kybernetes.* 1 (1972) 79-85.

12. R. Pestel, *Eine neue, umfassende Methodologie für die Technologische Folgeabschätzung aufgrund der Theorie der hierarchischen Mehrebenensysteme* (Hannover 1973), p. 11.

13. See H. Bossel, *Simulation des Normenstratums und des Normenwandels am Beispiel des Verhältnisses zwischen Entwicklungsland und Industrieland.* (Karlsruhe: Institut für Systemtechnik und Innovationsforschung, March 1973).

14. See, e.g., M. Mesarovic, E. Pestel et al., *An Interactive Decision Stratum for the Multilevel World Model*, Multilevel World Model Project, (Hannover: Technical University, Report no. 3, January 1973). Further, the same authors' *An Implementation of the World Economic System Model*, vols. 1 and 2 (Hannover, July 1973).

15. See A. Anné, "Comments on 'Similarities and Differences Between Control Systems in Engineering and Biology': State Variable Approach to the Analysis of Biological Systems," in *Global Systems Dynamics*, edited by E.O. Attinger (Basle, Munich, New York 1970).

Chapter Four

The Transformation

OVERCOMING THE STRUCTURES OF DOMINANCE

We are moving in the direction of increasing entropy. The economic struggle concerns the exploitation of the downward entropic trend. This process of total economization paradoxically accelerates the increase of entropy, however. The more intensive and thorough the competitive struggle, the stronger capital's utilization tendency becomes and the more the process of entropization of the system is advanced. This phenomenon can be observed in the large areas under cultivation in Canada or in the overzealous deforestation in the developing countries. The consequences are ecological catastrophes, which are not limited solely to the industrial countries but occur, as experience shows today, at least as often, if not more so, in the developing countries. The maneuverability and problem-solving capacity of the international system are therefore rapidly decreasing. As Geoffrey Vickers succinctly put it, "we have created an ungovernable world."[1]

In place of the self-adaptive equilibrium processes which are being more and more completely destroyed by this development, administrative regulations and massive restrictions have appeared, all of which are supposed to help avoid the consequences of the ecology crisis. The developed industrial nations have a much larger potential for shifting the burden of responsibility during this process than the developing countries do. The industrial nations are the "rulers who set the rules" which determine the number of options available for accommodation. Within the realm of these ordering principles set up by the "rulers," the energy input created by the release of energies bound in the system operates to create structure and to display power. If one examines economic processes in connection with increasing entropy within the total system, one can see their evolutionary relevance.

These processes lead therefore to the formation of divergences and dependencies as well as to dominance relationships. The more the production process functions contrary to the minimum ecological conditions, the more these tensions come into play in every society with a high energy input at its disposal. This means nothing more than that the application of the most advanced scientific measures will continually increase the production process' rationality, effectiveness and efficiency, which will in turn result in self-reinforcing ruling circles as generators of powers. It has been pointed out that, for example, the consumption of raw materials per capita in the USA is 40 times the level in the developing countries. With energy consumption the proportions are even more unbalanced—1 to 100. Figure 4–1 illustrates these phenomena.

The efforts to reduce entropy are indirectly observable through the release of latent energy; this is the energetic basis for all economic processes. If one wants to reduce the resulting divergencies and concentrations of economic power and the accompanying economic and political dominance structures, one can theoretically accomplish this end only by curtailing capital's self-generating drive—that is, by de-economizing the entire process.

Today the exact opposite occurs during the process of the artificial production of needs in the industrial nations of the West. The vectorial technologies economically oriented to the self-generating reproduction of capital therefore come into increasing conflict with ecological constraints. We are clearly dealing with positive feedbacks here, to which, in the last analysis, the so-called growth drive can be traced. The process will be intensified due to the fact that the participants in the international systems do not as yet totally comprehend these connections and therefore do not have them under control.

We know that a complex system can only function if it is hierarchically structured. Hierarchical structures degenerate into dominance relationships only if a subsystem overshoots the limits set by a higher order. One must very clearly point out here that the self-generating drive of capital associated with the profit system threatens to burst the limits of the ecosystem as much as the planning mechanism of the socialistic economic system oriented to consumption and production does. Both systems produce dependency and dominating relationships. The economic growth process is an underlying factor in the drive for growth in both the privately

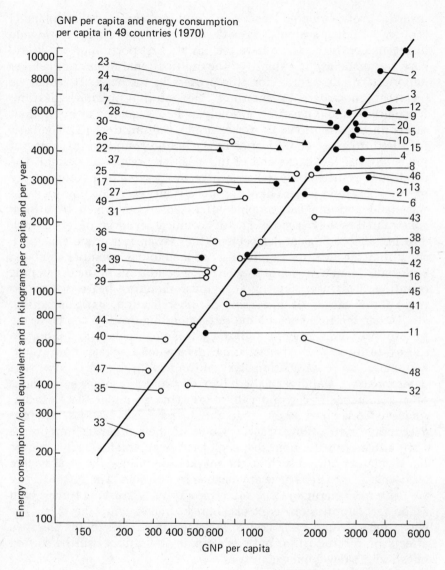

GNP per capita and energy consumption
per capita in 49 countries (1970)

Figure 4-1.

● North America, Western Europe,
  Oceania
▲ USSR and socialist countries in
  Eastern Europe
○ Latin America, Nonsocialist
  countries in Asia and South Africa

owned profit-oriented economy and in the socialist planned economy. Both systems' growth drive still produces worldwide divergencies which, as we have seen in the first portion of our study, have the tendency to intensify. The multinational firms are the most important driving force for this process in the West. It would be incorrect, however, to interpret the resulting peripheralization, fragmentation and penetration solely as a consequence or by-product of exploitive intentions, as, for example, Galtung does.[2] The basis for such processes could just as easily be the complete ignorance of the ecological feedbacks and of the sensitivity of the ecosystem. The conditions south of the Sahara where overgrazing and incorrect use of the ground water have produced an everwidening belt of wasteland and the catastrophic effects of dams which have been constructed solely according to technical criteria of efficiency, ignoring the ecological perspective (the Aswan is a prime example), show that the incorrect application of technology, whether capitalist or socialist, can contribute to worsening conditions in the developing countries. This use of technology must therefore be recognized as one of the causes of increasing peripheralization, marginalization, etc. Under the influence of the self-generating drive of capital in the private economic system and the advancing socialistic "shortrun-success-technology," the existing divergencies widen both internationally and intranationally. Autonomy, self-realization, self-determination, stability, justice, harmony and any other expressions of a dominance-free world cannot be achieved under these circumstances. Today we know that the hierarchical systems will not degenerate into ruling structures only if their ordering function is compatible with the objective ecological requirements. Only then do the regulatory forces such as the market, the prices, the legal system and other institutions have any chance to function. The further away we drift from harmony, the more rapidly the disturbing forces, such as power, suppression, controls, bureaucracies, will take over. The alienation of man and nature will then increase and the negative effects of the industrial nations' growth limitations will be shifted onto today's developing countries.

The central question thus arises: How can these disastrous processes be halted? One solution would involve the organization of a survival-oriented inclusion of man in the evolutionary process. The simultaneous maximization of options and of the subsystems' freedom will produce an evolutionarily adequate ethic which, in our historical situation, will lead to a worldwide de-economizing of material processes. Voluntary curtailment will result, as well as an end to the consumer society; codification of norms will be made possible through new institutions capable of learning, and through scientific analysis of the system's interconnections with the simultaneous broad participation of the public. In his treatise on the aftermath of the Stockholm Conference, Morris Strong expressed the hope that the United States would be in the position to construct an institutional network for an effective ecology management that would be flexible enough to engineer worldwide cooperation between nations. In this connection, he speaks of "managing the technological society at the international level."[3] The success of such a worldwide effort will require a radical change in values, however—that is to say, an ethic which on the basis of enlightened self-interest would also make possible the conclusion of an international nonproliferation treaty in the economic realm.

It is conceivable that these concepts are highly utopian. We still have very clear indications, however, that today people are working and thinking in this direction. The attempts to examine the inter- and intranational system as an analog to biological evolution are particularly interesting.[4] In this connection we should also mention the "World Order Models Project" (WOMP) which is presently proceeding under the direction of Professor Mendlovitz with the cooperation of several research institutes. This project attempts to present possible world orders which, in the view of various academic circles, should be discussed as "preferential structures." It has been planned to present these "realistic utopias" to a wide audience through the use of mass media and thereby to begin a process of participation which will be as broadly based as possible on a world scale and which will serve as an information pool for the further development of these models. It is in precisely the areas of disagreement where the options still available to the world community should be explained. There are different opinions as to the practical significance of such attempts, but just the fact that such attempts are being made gives reason for hope.[5]

With this background, China's importance in the world destiny becomes clear. We know that since her entrance into world politics, China has clearly understood her role to be the champion of the interests of the oppressed, the exploited and those discriminated against. She claims that she is not a superpower, but is rather a promoter of the liberation movements directed against these superpowers. In the short run, no definitive results can be expected from this stance, but in the long run it is conceivable that China, on the basis of her thousands of years of history, could be in the position of pointing out new developmental alternatives which will lead away from the destructive growth drives and make possible a societal existence which is compatible with the environment and, therefore, in the long run is stable.

ON THE WAY—WHERE?

Never before in the history of mankind have there been so many predictions about the future development of our society and never have the opinions about future prospects varied as widely as they do today. On one side stand the optimists who want us to believe that with the broadening of our knowledge and our technical capacities we will be in the position not only to continue material progress, but also to cope with its negative side effects. Training facilities will increase; we will learn to control population growth; social policy will be more effectively and rationally managed; industrialization, automation, specialization, real wages, leisure time, life expectancy, etc., etc., will all rise and will finally produce, particularly in conjunction with the increasing importance of services, a phenomenal increase in our income and therefore in our prosperity. More and more skeptical voices are being heard on the other side of this issue today—and with good reason. This technical-economic advancement has abolished basic poverty from one-third of the world; never have so many human beings had so much to eat, enjoyed so many educational opportunities or owned so many material goods, and never has the working time for this third of mankind been so short as it is today. Paradoxically, the exact opposite is also true. Never have there been so many people who are starving, who have no housing, no medical care, and who must exist in the most wretched circumstances. While one-third of mankind suffers from overfeeding and overproduction, all the industrial countries' technical and scientific advances have not been able to satisfy even the basic needs of the rest of the world. While industrial development turns more and more to the production of artificial needs in order to tap new markets for the self-generating drive of capital, the growing misery in the rest of the world cannot be checked.

The enormous display of human productive forces remained, up to now, limited to a few centers and was there pushed to the final limits of the ecosystem's carrying capacity. The principle of the expansion of investment and consumer goods industries aiming at a further rise in the material standard of living also rules in the camp of the so-called socialist industrial countries. In the one camp, the technical economic expansive forces are basically regulated and operated through the market mechanism of a private economic system. In the other camp, seen from the outside, these forces are the result of a controlled planning process. A pronounced drive for growth is inherent in both systems, although for different reasons. Under capitalistic production requirements, any reduction in the growth rate can lead to serious disturbances in the production process, while any limitations on the development of the human productive forces stand in direct conflict with Marxist ideology.

The uneasiness concerning this snowballing acceleration of all production processes and, above all, concerning the increasing absurdity of a system dependent upon the production of artificial needs, has spread—particularly within the Western industrial nations —in the last few years. The advances in instrumental knowledge have extended our know-how into unthought of dimensions. In relation to our "know-what," however, we have made practically no progress. This development is not surprising to anthropologists, psychologists and sociologists. They have long been aware that this phenomenal expansion of material productive forces goes hand in hand with the equally rapid destruction of our moral and ethical bases, which are at least as important for the proper functioning and survival of a society as the availability of material goods is. The Western industrial civilization has thus produced a consumer-human who is neither willing nor in the position to make a contribution in the form of a reduction in his levels of aspirations. The system encourages and rewards only those activities which contribute to a rising level of productivity allowing more leisure time and more consumption according to pure market economy principles.[6]

The situation briefly outlined here has primarily led to a flood of publications concerned with the major question of where we should be and where we are heading. The American government created the National Goals Research Staff in 1970 which was supposed to investigate the problem of economic growth in terms of quantity and quality.[7] The staff began with a simple question: If we raise our income 50 percent in the next ten years, will we be 50 percent better off or 50 percent happier? This impressive report provides valuable information on a number of basic problems such as urbanization, science's new role, education, the restoration of the already damaged environment and technology assessment. In contrast to discussions during the sixties, when people still believed they could clearly set specific goals, this report points out the remaining available options. It states that we must learn to anticipate our problems and to consider carefully and systematically the existing possibilities. As this report astutely observes, we are mere neophytes at anticipatory decisionmaking.

Stated very simplistically, the Western industrial societies find themselves increasingly insecure and perplexed, while the official party in the socialist industrial countries still proclaims a remarkably positive and optimistic production ideology which is forced upon its subjects as the basic content of their lives through a completely bureaucratic control of the accomplishment of their plans. The unavoidable result for both the Western and the socialist industrial countries is a human being reduced to the property of a seemingly meaningless drive for growth, one who is alienated from the system and who would like to break out of it. In order to accomplish this, he paradoxically employs the very technical means which were produced by this development.

This alienation has produced, for example, more than 2,000 communes in the United States; they have established themselves in very different milieus outside of this compulsively technical, civilizing system. Agricultural, craft-oriented and political communes, to give just a sampling, exist in almost every state in the United States and produce a total of over 200 underground newspapers, 50 magazines and their own telephone books and address listings. They operate a total of 500 schools, 300 "human growth and development centers" and 250 so-called "free clinics." These countercultural groups are rapidly increasing in the United States and form a growing reservoir for models of alternative societies. In order to be able to realize their aims, these groups nonetheless remain somewhat dependent upon the technical infrastructure which industrialism has produced. As recent investigations have shown, however, certain groups have already succeeded in creating an economic basis for the achievement of their cultural self-realization. This is probably the first time in the history of industrial civilization that it has been possible to create niches which could later become vital centers for relief from the otherwise unbearable side effects of technical civilization. Without wishing to overestimate the significance of these "alternative living areas," one can discover a very real alternative to the otherwise conventional utopias offered up to now by philosophers such as Huxley, Toynbee or Herman Kahn. Encouragingly enough, many scientific investigations of this phenomenon are already available.[8] Among the different groups' magazines and catalogues, the following bear mention: *Alternatives Journal, Communities, Ed Centric, Life Styles, New Schools Exchange Newsletter, Source* and *Work Force*.

It seems that the American society of today, in spite of, or perhaps due to, its hypertrophic industrialsim, has made much more progress in the direction of delineation of alternatives than, say, the Soviet society. In Russia, every movement of this sort is almost automatically viewed as dissident, subversive to socialism, useless and parasitic, all which will inevitably lead to bans on such activity. While such subcultures are tolerated in the Western industrial nations as long as they do not lead to criminal acts, the Soviet Union has no idea as yet of how to deal with these developments which will sooner or later also crop up within their environs.

The particular significance of these societal-ecological niches lies not only in their function as oases, but also in the fact that they point out a way to realize a highly differentiated societal system consistent with the environment. With the incorporation of technical means of communication, this system would permit a high degree of self-realization and an individual freedom within small, clearly arranged subsystems. It would be easier to achieve an evolutionarily adequate ethic within such subsystems than within the framework of the classical, large national state in which, as we have seen, the endogenic regulatory forces deteriorate and must be replaced by bureaucratic controls, often at the expense of individual freedoms. Here the massive problem area for the "Where are we going?" of our development can be pinpointed: Growth limitation is inseparably connected with the new conception of the state and the creation of space for the realization of ideas in which independent cultures can develop and can form a network within a larger territorial association, possibly beyond today's national boundaries. Conover correctly points out that, for many experts, the national state, examined in terms of ecological and cultural data, is an artificial form: from an ecological standpoint, national boundaries are insane; they divide cultures, separate humans who have a common interest, force totally different cultures into one unit and into the same national area and subject them all to the same legal system. There are innumerable examples of the position allotted to the minority groups in various nations. The Aborigines in Australia, the Indians in North America, the Bantus in South Africa, the Kurden in Iraq, the LaCandonen in Southern Mexico, the Pygmies in Central Africa, the Chakma in Bangladesh, the Puerto Ricans in New York, the Tamilen in Sri Lanka — all are underprivileged groups who must live under a form of organization basically alien to them and who are seen either as a potential threat or as the object of exploitation. The nation states have not yet learned to cope with these problems, but here is one of our greatest opportunities for the future. If we can succeed in providing these subcultures already in existence with the organizational, technical and economic requirements for their self-realization, we will be able to reduce conflicts which otherwise would certainly occur during the process of growth limitation and which would result in an escalation in national measures of restraint toward these groups. The almost universal curtailment of free presses today is an index of the increasing difficulties which the nation state is facing as it performs its controlling functions.

We now arrive at several basic questions about the function of national states which are important to the future of the state system. A connection exists between the size of the state, territorially speaking, its degree of material dependence and the successful identification of the citizenry with the goals of their state. After a certain point in industrial development, one can say that states with a large amount of territory are, in principle, economically independent. The minimal significance of foreign trade to economies like the USA or the Soviet Union clearly illustrates this point. Smaller nations depend more upon foreign trade; they cannot be self-sufficient.

In comparison to the large countries, however, the more compact relationships possible in a small country generally give rise to more clarity, to a more intensive communication between the government and the people. Think, for example, about countries like Switzerland or the Netherlands. They can offer the possibility of a larger solidarity between the population and the state institutions, including the government, which is at least partially controlled by the citizens. One could never expect such harmony within the larger nations, and since these nations generally wield substantial military and economic power, they pose a threat to the smaller nations to the degree that the larger nations are able to shift their own conflicts one way or another onto these smaller countries. In the light of the intensifying drive toward growth limitation, it would be most desirable for the stability of the international system to have as many small nations as possible. Unfortunately, the large nations, presiding over impressive military and economic power, will not allow themselves to be splintered out of existence. It would be wonderful if one could claim the same resiliency for today's subcultures and minorities. Although it becomes increasingly difficult to liquidate such groups without having the rest of the world realize what is happening, the nation state has enough means at its disposal— without being a superpower—to deport or even liquidate undesirable minorities or members of alternative cultures under one pretext or another.

These groups' survival will depend decisively upon whether or not the large territorial nations recognize in time that the existence of such subcultures is highly important for the transition from economic-technical to societal-human growth. These groups not only provide relief from the unbearable side effects of technical civilization; they also serve primarily to promote practical possibilities for real alternatives on a generally low level of economic activity. This movement is highly relevant to growth limitation. If the path toward decentralization and the support of subcultures cannot be followed—assuming that the policy of growth limitation will continue to be pursued—social conflicts of unimaginable dimensions will ensue and the national and international class struggle will intensify sharply.[9]

THE CRITICAL PHASES

As I began to write the final section of this book, the fourth Middle East conflict broke out. The events since then have demonstrated the solidity of the American-Soviet détente mentioned in the first chapter. If any further proof were needed for the dominance of these two superpowers, this extraordinarily difficult international situation has provided it. Both the Soviet Union and the United States have practiced highly effective crisis management over the heads of their allies and then engaged the UN Security Council, over China's protest, to support the ordering function they had assumed. As much as one must applaud the results of these efforts, one cannot avoid drawing parallels with those theories which point out the dangers of this hegemonial bipolarity. It would therefore be false to deduce from the present uneasy peace engineered by the two superpowers that from now on world peace is assured. At least two circumstances militate against such assumptions: (1) With the increasing world disparities, the pent-up conflict potential is more likely than ever to explode under the "umbrella" of one of the superpowers' ordering functions, because now people will proceed on the premise that the danger of an uncontrolled acceleration toward an all-encompassing nuclear war is no longer as large. (2) The atomic armament and further development of new weapons systems will continue at full speed in both the USA and the Soviet Union despite the SALT talks. The major priorities in both countries will emphasize rocket troops, the Navy and the Air Force. It is an open secret that the SALT talks will not only not slow down the development of new systems or the improvement of existing systems, but that it will actually encourage such progress. It is also no secret that the Soviet Union leads today in the area of tactical guided missiles for sea battle. The development of new guided missiles revolutionized naval warfare for the Soviets. This is not the place to conduct a thorough investigation of the two superpowers' strategic weapon systems. The *Strategic Survey* of the International Institute for Strategic Studies in London, published annually, provides a good overview of the current state of armament and of any new developments.

One characteristic feature of the armament race is, as Lambelet,[10] among others, pointed out in a very informative study, the *instability* of the two superpowers' intimidation system developed by the armament race. This instability will be increased by the effectiveness of the armament process' endogenic self-dynamic within the two great powers [11] as well as by the incongruence of the American and Soviet strategic concepts.[12] While, as Iklé states, American strategy is still based on the concept of nuclear deterrence, the Soviets do not seem to share this rather limited position unconditionally any longer, thereby developing a more encompassing, long term and flexible concept. Nuclear deterrence is included as one of many possibilities within this strategy. It is possible that this expanded concept will lead to a new era of indirect strategy in which military factors do not play the only determining role. The strategy anticipates a large number of long term conflicts and, moving beyond the military realm, concerns itself with the world's total societal-political development. This strategy can therefore deal with events outside of the classical bipolarity such as (1) China's rapidly increasing nuclear potential and (2) the inevitable proliferation of nuclear weapons outside of the five established nuclear powers.

Following the increased plutonium production and the chance to enrich uranium, it appears that certain nations will soon be able to produce nuclear weapons. The international Atomic Energy Organization has just lately begun to deal with this problem, but has had to limit itself to recommendations for protective measures which will be provided at the request of the member nations. The Strategic Survey of 1970 listed all the nations outside of the nuclear powers who either had their own enrichment plants for uranium or the technical expertise to build them. These included Belgium, Argentina, West Germany, India, Italy, Spain, Japan, Canada, Norway, Sweden and the Netherlands, of which Argentina, India and Spain had not signed the Nonproliferation Treaty. It is also very easy to foresee that we will soon experience a booming world trade in atomic weapons. If one recalls that as a result of the increased demand for petroleum and the astronomical price tags, the oil-producing countries will have huge sums of money on hand, it does not take much imagination to predict the consequences. It is more than questionable whether under these circumstances the critical transition from a bipolar power confrontation to a network of multipolar relationships can be successfully achieved. Seyom Brown outlines a plan which must be followed by the large powers if there is to be any hope for a new international system:

1. ... the two military superpowers [must] not utilize their military superiority, even as an implicit bargaining chip, in order to influence weaker military participants ...
2. ... the largest, strongest and wealthiest countries will have to refrain from attempting to maintain or establish spheres of dominance. ... Such "hegemonial multipolarity" is inherently unstable ... and would lead to conflicts.
3. ... the leading economic and technological nations ... will have to ... actively encourage the elaboration of multiple and intersecting webs of interdependence between [all] countries. ...
4. ... the world's political economy will have to be restructured to implement redistributive interferences in the global market ....
5. ... to prevent misuse of and conflicts over the world's common resources ... new sets of representative institutions will need to be elaborated and empowered on regional and global bases to ensure that all the communities affected have a fair say over how these common goods of mankind are used.[14]

One has a tendency to say: I hear the message; I just don't believe it. When one sees the machinations of the multinational firms, how people haggle about the slightest benefits in the realm of the EEC, how national self-interest destroyed the international currency system and with what methods the powerful nations are monopolizing raw materials, one hardly feels inclined to view Seyom Brown's well-intended resolutions as particularly realistic ones.

Shortly after he had been named Mao Tse-tung's successor in 1965, Lin Piao drew a very different picture of the future development of the international system. He said that one could consider the rich industrial nations of North America and Europe as "cities" which are surrounded by the countryside in which the large underprivileged masses of the Third World live. Just as the countryside ultimately took over the cities during the Chinese Revolution, the masses of underprivileged in Asia, Africa and Latin America will also triumph over the industrial nations. This analogy may seem too "Chinese," too allegorical, but its aggressive tone is probably more realistic than Seyom Brown's moralistic catalogue.

Let us summarize: The transition from the superpowers' hegemonial dominance system to a militarily, economically and politically well-balanced world system can only be achieved, if at all, by the powerful nations' self-restraint in their use of power.

HOW MUCH TIME DO WE STILL HAVE?

There is only one answer to this question—a little, very little—but that does not explain the whole situation. The philosopher, Jeanne Hersch, once said that nature's time structure is fundamentally different from man's. Time experienced by man is not continuous; he has a "before" and "after" as well as a "now." This philosophical view points to a fact of basic importance to man's existence and survival. This situation can be clearly seen if one breaks "nature" into components which belong to different time dimensions according to their rapidity of change.

Table 4–1 illustrates a comparison of components and time dimensions in the natural and societal systems. Such a comparison would be rather uninteresting if the changes in these systems occurred completely independently of each other. The central time problem for man's existence, however, derives directly from the state of dependence man has created between these different rates of change. Let us examine a few examples:

Within a relatively few years, man has burned up fossil materials which took several hundred million years to form.

Radioactive fallout has a half-life of several thousand years; social structures controlled by man have a life expectancy of a maximum of hundreds of years.

Genetic manipulations has been made possible by the accumulation of scientific knowledge over a few decades; the effects of such manipulation could be irreversible.

Table 4–1.

Type of systems and processes	Time dimensions in which changes of systems occur (years)*
geological processes	10^4 to 10^9
biological processes	less than 10^9
complex forms of life	$550 \cdot 10^6$
development of the neo cortex	3.10^4 to 10^5
ecological processes	10 to 10^4
economic processes	decades
political processes	e.g., the average length of the legislative period (in most cases four to five years); life expectancy of dictatorships 0 to 40 years.
technical processes	1 to 20
human organism	0 to 70

*10^4 = 10000. 10^6 = 1 million; 10^9 = 1 billion.

Ecosystems reach their dynamic equilibria within a thousand year period. The disturbances caused by people, for example in the global thermal balance, appear suddenly, within a few decades.

Economic growth produces tangible results within decades; the average life of a government is only a few years.

Material changes triggered by man develop much more quickly than man's ability to adjust his behavior with new norms and values.

One could offer further, similar examples. Ernst Basler converted the speed of evolution in the natural environment to a human time scale in his very informative book, *Strategie des Fortschritts (Strategy for Advancement)*.[15] Basler's comparison is so striking that we have quoted him extensively. He begins thus:

If we could compress the last 170 million years of natural history into one year, in order to gain a perspective on the speed of the natural evolution process, a scenario of progress would look something like this:

in January of our model year, we find the terrestial continental land masses already covered with a thick layer of vegetation, and the evolution of the so-called mammals begins. In March the first species of bird appear, in May new deciduous trees, such as figs, magnolias and poplars. July brings the high point in the development of the giant reptiles, but toward September they die out, as do the dinosaurs. In October the development of the primates begins, and in the second week in November the development of the anthropoid apes. Between Christmas and New Year our ancestors appear, walking upright and using stone tools. On December 31, at 10 PM, the Neanderthal group dies out.

30 minutes before midnight, something begins which has never been there previously; a decisive threshold is crossed. An earth species—namely, *homo sapiens*—begins to actively influence the natural surface of the earth: he has freed himself of an existence of mere hunting, collecting and passive harvesting.

... 18 minutes before midnight the wooden wheel is invented; the bronze alloy, lightning rod and steam engine are constructed later, at 36 seconds before midnight. The automobile appears at 13 and the airplane at 12 seconds before midnight. DDT was discovered seconds before twelve, the washing materials containing phosphates were put on the market at 11:56, and today—that is, punctually at midnight on December 31 of our model year—we have reached a speed of advancement which doubles the total amount of manmade civilized goods every 4 seconds.[16]

The time problem thus derives from the "speed of advancement," which is several times as large as the time dimensions in which, for example, the neocortex of the *homo sapiens*, which controls the higher functions of the brain, developed. An "adjustment deficit" in man's behavior necessarily results; man finds himself today in a frustrating race with time. The formation of an evolutionarily adequate ethic cannot keep pace with the effects of the civilization processes stimulated by man's "rationality." In his important treatise, "Ueber die genetische Zukunft des Menschen" ("Concerning Man's Genetic Future"), H. Baitsch remarked:

> Above all, however, we will have to pursue environmental research more intensively than ever before, with the goal of recognizing the environmental factors created by mankind which overtax, partially or completely, the hereditarily determined reaction norms in the blueprints for the species man, so that we can correct these factors. At the same time it will be decisively important to know how large a variety exists in these human reaction norms; our knowledge here is still insufficient.[17]

The biological evolution of man occurs in totally different time dimensions from those in which the human-triggered environmental changes do. The mainspring for these changes is the technical-economic rationale, along with its value system which, viewed in terms of evolutionary history, has spread over the entire earth within "a few seconds." Both the people and their aspirations are growing, and the rationally organized economic systems support short term "material drives" which will all contribute to the drive for growth. The more pronounced man's adjustment difficulties become during this process, the more frantically he searches for short term, instant measures to be implemented with technical means, while on the other end of the scale he has made no—or cannot make any—adjustments in his norms and values.

We are shortsighted, have no management sense, react incorrectly and pay too much attention to superficialities. This situation arises from the fact that we only look at the world in its physical, evolutionary and societal dimensions through "windows"—that is, in segments. Every highschooler knows that our eye can register only a small segment of the total range of electromagnetic waves as light, that our ear can hear tones only up to approximately $12,000$ H_z and that we cannot positively conceptualize a distance of a million light years. It is less well known that we are able to perceive only fragments of the complex technical-societal network of today's civilization. The human brain can follow the interaction of a maximum of five to seven variables in a system, and even that can, according to the nature of the interaction, be too much. In reality, however, technical-economic systems are composed of thousands of elements which all interconnect somehow and influence each other.

For the first time, only very recently, new methods of computer-oriented simulation have allowed a broadening of our field of vision. Compared to the complexity of the technical-economic system of which we form one part, they still provide only small peepholes through which we can peer.

What, then, should we do? What *can* we do? Two measures could help here:

One measure is *decentralization*—that is, the creation of clear relationships. This leads in the direction of subsystems which have been previously mentioned. Instead of squandering our research capacities on new, more rapid airplanes, cars, etc., in the future we will have to deal much more intensively with the theory and implementation of homeostatic societal systems. Research in this area is still in the initial stages; the "naturally" developing subsystems (subcultures) are considered burdens or even threats and are eliminated wherever possible.

The second measure involves curbing the self-generating, *inflationary demand* in the rich industrial nations. This control concerns not only consumer demand, but also demands upon the productive potential of the technical systems. That means that technology can no longer be judged according to its own criteria of efficiency, but must be considered as a component in a biologically organized whole. Technology assessment is a first step in this direction.

How much time do we therefore still have? As I said at the beginning, very little. If man considers that decentralization and changes in our attitudes toward consumption and technology also require time, it seems questionable whether or not we will survive the time pressure. Man has, as Cramer impressively demonstrates,[18] fundamentally changed the requirements for his biological evolution in the Darwinian sense. Is he also politically outside the evolution?

Man has not developed any growth-limiting consciousness either as an individual or in a societal group. This differentiates him from all other natural organizations except for cancerous cells. Basic anthropological research will have to work with system theories and biological research will have to work toward a *swift* change in the values and aspirations of man *and* nations so that they can be adapted to the ecosystem's circular processes before it is too late—that is, before the stabilizing cycles are completely destroyed by the uncontrolled vectorial process of the civilization. The time available for this end can be measured, at a maximum, in *decades*, assuming that we succeed in using schools and adult education to effectively influence all age levels.

NOTES

1. Geoffrey Vickers, *Freedom in a Rocking Boat* (Middlesex: Pelican Books 1972), p. 123.

2. See Johan Galtung, "The Limits to Growth and Class Politics," (Oslo: International Peace Research Institute, 1973), manuscript.

3. See M. F. Strong, "One Year After Stockholm. An Ecological Approach to Management," *Foreign Affairs* 51,4 (July 1973): 707.

4. See, e.g., Claude S. Philipps, Jr., "Biology, Cultural Evolution, and the Political Process." (Paper prepared for the 1973 Annual Meeting of the International Political Science Association, Montreal).

5. See the publications of the Institute for World Order, Inc., 11 West 42nd Street, New York, N.Y. 10036.

6. See for example, E. Küng, "Wohin geht die gesellschaftliche Entwicklung? Konsequenzen für die Wirtschaft," *Volkswirtschaftliche Korrespondenz der Adolf-Weber-Stiftung*, no. 4, 1973.

7. *Toward Balanced Growth: Quantity with Quality*. Report of the National Goals Research Staff (Washington, D.C.: US Government Printing Office, 1970).

8. See, for example, P.W. Conover, "The Potential for an Alternate Society," *The Futurist*, VII, 3 (June 1973); Richard Fairfield, *Communes U.S.A.*, (Baltimore: Penguin, 1971); Robert J. Glessing, *The Underground Press in America* (Bloomington: Indiana University Press, 1971); William Hedgepeth and Dennis Stock, *The Alternative-Communal Life in New America* (New York: Macmillan, 1970); Rosabeth M. Kanter, *Commitment and Community* (Cambridge, Mass.: Harvard University Press, 1972); Jonathan Kozol, *Free Schools* (Boston: Houghton-Mifflin, 1972); Ron E. Roberts, *The New Communes* (Englewood Cliffs, N.J.: Prentice-Hall, 1971); Theodore Roszak, *The Making of a Counter Culture* (Garden City, N.Y.: Doubleday-Anchor, 1969); Benjamin Zablocki, *The Joyful Community* (Baltimore: Penguin, 1971); Twin Oaks Community, "Experimenting With Walden Two" (Louisa, 1972).

9. See G. Bombach, "Planspiele zum Ueberleben," *Mitteilungen der List Gesellschaft*, facs. 8, no. 1, 1973.

10. J.C. Lambelet, "Towards a Dynamic Two-Theatre Model of the East-West Arms Race" (University of Pennsylvania and University of Lausanne, Research Paper Manuscript, 1973).

11. See D. Senghaas, "The Impact of Domestic Interests and National Decision Systems in the Post-1945 Arms Race: Some Reflexions on Armament Dynamics" (Paper presented at the IXth World Congress of the International Political Science Association, Montreal 1973).

12. See F.Ch. Iklé, "Can Nuclear Deterrence Last out the Century?" *Foreign Affairs* 51, 2 (1973): 267–285.

13. See A. Beaufre, *Die Revolutionierung des Kriegsbildes—Neue Formen der Gewaltanwendung* (Stuttgart, 1973).

14. Seyom Brown, "The Changing Essence of Power," *Foreign Affairs* 51, 2 (1973).

15. See E. Basler, *Strategie des Fortschritts* (Frauenfeld and Stuttgart, 1972).

16. Ibid., pp. 15f.

17. See H. Baitsch, "Ueber die genetische Zukunft des Menschen," *Universitas* 28. 8 (1973): 826.

18. See F. Cramer, "Fortschritt: Natur contra Kultur?" *gdi-topics* 3. 10 (November 1972): 3–10.

Conclusion

There are no pat solutions to the problems outlined in this book; one cannot maintain that we face certain destruction, but our hope for a harmonious world also cannot come close to certainty. The drive toward growth limitation can lead to attempts at a high technological-economic level to avoid responsibility for the ultimate problems; this would merely establish a new form of exploitation and create new polarizations. The same drive, however, can awake the strongest industrial nations to their global responsibility and lead to a worldwide effort. Theoretically, all possibilities are open, even though we cannot rule out the probability, given all that we have observed, that growth limitation will become an instrument of power. Nonetheless, the range of possibilities is still so large that it leaves room for hope and luck—and also for danger. History has an open agenda; within limits our value systems can be changed. Only a few years ago the Western industrial societies were still caught up in an almost boundless euphoria of growth. Today we are not only aware of the limitations to our power, our wealth and our technology; we are now also beginning to recognize the limits to our room for adjustment as well as to the control and dominance we can exercise over our societal-technical system. There is hope in the fact that today societal needs, projected goals and possible consequences are undergoing critical consideration and discussion. We are less positivistic today than we were a few years ago. This change of consciousness is no longer limited to a small group of specialists; it encompasses larger and larger segments of the population. The way toward a new evaluation of short term advantages versus long term dangers in thoughtless economic growth has thereby opened up. We therefore at least have the chance politically to actualize a set of priorities which are compatible with the requirements of a long term equilibrium.

In evaluating this hopeful consciousness change one should not overlook the dangers which threaten us on all sides. We have not yet learned to regulate technology's inherent dynamics which are driven by military and economic forces. Today the danger of expansion of nuclear weapons is larger than ever and the societal consequences of accelerating technical developments in the areas of data processing, automation, sales promotion, technology transfer and observation with satellites cannot be imagined.

Before we can begin to analyze the consequences of such developments, technical progress has advanced several steps further. We are uneasy about such phenomena, but we have not yet succeeded in controlling these propelling forces and releasing them at a level suited to the human capacity to adjust. Technical development is running away from us, and every advance in technical manipulation makes the societal system as a whole more uncontrollable. It is technical efficiency measured by its own criteria which makes our societal and political steering mechanisms unusable. In a world of technical wonders we are paradoxically caught in a situation in which the regulatory forces are largely disconnected—due in large part to these autonomous technical developments. This produces a very dangerous situation on an international level. The nations are the decisive factors; their behavior will decide the future of the global system. If the maneuverability of a state is reduced by the destruction of its inner regulatory forces, it will be almost impossible to conceive of a general policy commensurate with the global dependencies on an international level. Because of such uncontrolled, and in this situation uncontrollable, processes, conflicts which would also be unmanageable could arise at very little provocation.

Cramer says with great logic that the end to advancement can only be brought about, "if all human beings and political groups decide simultaneously and together that they now have enough. This "social contract" of a higher order would have to be an all-encompassing nonproliferation treaty which extended itself not only to atom bombs but also to energy production, population growth, medical research and waste production."[1] How can we bring such a nonproliferation treaty into being on an international scale when the elements constituting the international system—namely, the nations themselves—are experiencing an advancing destruction of their own regulatory powers? We come face to face with a fundamental dilemma here: On the one hand, domestic growth limitation without endangering a nation's own position is possible only on the basis of an international "growth ban treaty." On the other hand, it will be almost impossible to conclude such a treaty because of the worldwide simultaneity necessitated by competitive factors. Even if such a miracle occurred, provisions for fair financial settlement between the industrial and developing countries would have to be included because of international development inequalities. One can easily imagine how small the chances would be for such an arrangement.

For all of these reasons—and one could add many more—one can consider such a nonproliferation treaty utopian. It is much more likely that bilateral associations between the great industrial powers will result and that they, by way of environmental policy, will lead to a mutual synchronization of growth rates without affecting these nations' preeminence in relation to the developing countries. We have shown that the core groups have the means to accomplish these ends.

The impossibility of a worldwide atomic war has left us with a Machiavellian peace. The impossibility of a worldwide growth waiver transforms the wealthy nations' growth limitation into an instrument of power which will leave the poor countries of the world completely helpless, despite China's support.

NOTES

1. F. Cramer, "Fortschritt: Natur contra Kultur?" *gdi-topics* 3, 10(November 1972): 9.

Text of the Washington Agreement for the Limitation of Strategic Offensive Arms: Basic Principles of Negotiations

Text of the Washington Agreement for the Limitation of Strategic Offensive Arms: Basic Principles of Negotiations

The President of the United States of America, Richard Nixon, and the General Secretary of the Central Committee of the CPSU, L.I. Brezhnev,

Having thoroughly considered the question of the further limitation of strategic arms, and the progress already achieved in the current negotiations,

Reaffirming their conviction that the earliest adoption of further limitations of strategic arms would be a major contribution in reducing the danger of an outbreak of nuclear war and in strengthening international peace and security,

Have agreed as follows:

First. The two sides will continue active negotiations in order to work out a permanent agreement on more complete measures on the limitation of strategic offensive arms, as well as their subsequent reduction, proceeding from the Basic Principles of Relations between the United States of America and the Union of Soviet Socialist Republics signed in Moscow on May 22, 1972, and from the Interim Agreement between the United States of America and the Union of Soviet Socialist Republics of May 26, 1972, on Certain Measures with Respect to the Limitation of Strategic Offensive Arms.

Over the course of the next year the two sides will make serious efforts to work out the provisions of the permanent agreement on more complete measures on the limitation of strategic offensive arms with the objective of signing it in 1974.

Second. New agreements on the limitation of strategic offensive armaments will be based on the principles of the American-Soviet documents adopted in Moscow in May 1972 and the agreements reached in Washington in June 1973; and in particular, both sides will be guided by the recognition of each other's equal security interests and by the recognition that efforts to obtain unilateral advantage, directly or indirectly, would be inconsistent with the strengthening of peaceful relations between the United States of America and the Union of Soviet Socialist Republics.

Third. The limitations placed on strategic offensive weapons can apply both to their quantitative aspects as well as to their qualitative improvement.

Fourth. Limitations on strategic offensive arms must be subject to adequate verification by national technical means.

Fifth. The modernization and replacement of strategic offensive arms would be permitted under conditions which will be formulated in the agreements to be concluded.

Sixth. Pending the completion of a permanent agreement on more complete measures of strategic offensive arms limitation, both Sides are prepared to reach agreements on separate measures to supplement the existing Interim Agreement of May 26, 1972.

Seventh. Each Side will continue to take necessary organizational and technical measures for preventing accidental or unauthorized use of nuclear weapons under its control in accordance with the Agreement of September 30, 1971, between the United States of America and the Union of Soviet Socialist Republics.

Agreement signed at Washington June 21, 1973;
Entered into force June 21, 1973.

Appendix B

Income Distribution Estimates

Percentage Shares in Total National Income Going to Population Groups of Different Income Levels in 44 Countries

	Poorest 0–20 Percent	Poorest 21–39 Percent	Middle 40–60 Percent	Highest 61–79 Percent	Highest 20 Percent	Highest 5 Percent
Argentina	7.00	10.30	13.10	17.60	52.00	29.40
Bolivia	4.00	13.70	8.90	14.30	59.10	35.70
Brazil	3.50	9.00	10.20	15.80	61.50	38.40
Burma	10.00	13.00	13.00	15.50	48.50	28.21
Chad	12.00	11.00	12.00	22.00	43.00	23.00
Chile	5.40	9.60	12.00	20.70	52.30	22.60
Colombia	2.21	4.70	8.97	16.06	68.06	40.36
Costa Rica	6.00	7.30	12.10	14.60	60.00	35.00
Dahomey	8.00	10.00	12.00	20.00	50.00	32.00
Ecuador	6.30	16.00	13.40	22.60	41.80	21.50
El Salvador	5.50	6.80	11.30	15.00	61.40	33.00
Gabon	2.00	6.00	7.00	14.00	71.00	47.00
Greece	9.00	12.80	12.30	16.40	49.50	23.00
India	8.00	12.00	16.00	12.00	42.00	20.00
Iraq	2.00	6.00	8.00	16.00	68.00	34.00
Israel	6.80	13.40	18.60	21.80	39.40	11.20
Ivory Coast	8.00	10.00	12.00	15.00	55.00	29.00
Jamaica	2.20	6.00	10.80	19.50	61.50	31.20
Japan	4.70	10.60	15.80	22.90	46.00	14.80
Kenya	7.00	7.00	7.00	15.00	64.00	22.20
Lebanon	3.00	4.20	15.80	16.00	61.00	34.00
Libya	0.11	0.39	1.28	8.72	89.50	46.40
Malagasy	7.00	7.00	9.00	18.00	59.00	37.00
Mexico	3.66	6.84	11.25	20.21	58.04	28.52

	Poorest 0–20 Percent	*Poorest 21–39 Percent*	*Middle 40–60 Percent*	*Highest 61–79 Percent*	*Highest 20 Percent*	*Highest 5 Percent*
Marocco	7.10	7.40	7.70	12.40	65.40	20.60
Niger	12.00	11.00	12.00	23.00	42.00	23.00
Nigeria	7.00	7.00	9.00	16.10	60.90	38.38
Pakistan	6.50	11.00	15.50	22.00	45.00	20.00
Panama	4.90	9.40	13.80	15.20	56.70	34.50
Peru	4.04	4.76	8.30	15.30	67.60	48.30
Philippines	4.30	8.40	12.00	19.50	55.80	27.50
Rhodesia	4.00	8.00	8.00	15.00	65.00	60.00
Senegal	3.00	7.00	10.00	16.00	64.00	36.00
Sierra Leone	3.80	6.30	9.10	16.70	64.10	33.80
South Africa	1.94	4.17	10.16	26.37	57.36	39.38
Sri Lanka (Ceylon)	4.45	9.21	13.81	20.22	52.31	18.38
Sudan	5.60	9.40	14.30	22.60	48.10	17.10
Surinam	10.70	11.56	14.74	20.60	42.40	15.40
Taiwan	4.50	9.70	14.80	19.00	52.00	24.10
Tanzania	9.75	9.65	9.85	9.75	61.00	42.90
Trinidad & Tobago	3.60	5.76	9.16	24.48	57.00	26.60
Tunisia	4.97	5.65	9.95	14.43	65.00	22.44
Venezuela	4.40	7.00	16.60	24.90	47.10	23.20
Zambia	6.27	9.58	11.10	15.95	57.10	37.50
Averages	5.60	8.40	12.00	17.71	56.00	30.00

Based on: E. Adelman and C.T. Morris "An Anatomy of Income Distribution Patterns in Developing Countries."

Appendix C

The 20 Largest Industrial Corporations 1971

Rank	Company	Country	Sales ($000)	Assets ($000)	Employees
1.	General Motors	US	28,264	18,242	773,352
2.	Standard Oil	US	18,701	20,315	143,000
3.	Ford Motor	US	16,433	10,510	433,074
4.	Royal Dutch/Shell	NE-GB	12,734	19.649	185,000
5.	General Electric	US	9,425	6,888	363,000
6.	IBM	US	8,274	9,576	265,493
7.	Mobil Oil	US	8,243	8,552	75,300
8.	Chrysler	US	7,999	5,000	227,397
9.	Texaco	US	7,529	10,933	75,192
10.	Unilever	GB-NE	7,483	4,449	324,000
11.	ITT	US	7,346	7,630	398,000
12.	Western Electric	US	6,045	4,012	207,015
13.	Gulf Oil	US	5,940	9,466	57,200
14.	BP	GB	5,191	7,867	70,600
15.	Philips	NE	5,189	6,543	367,000
16.	Standard Oil California	US	5,143	7,513	42,527
17.	VW	FRG	4,967	3,107	202,029
18.	US Steel	US	4,928	6,409	183,940
19.	Westinghouse	US	4,631	3,538	180,714
20.	Nippon Steel	Japan	4,088	9,114	100,821
	Total		178,553	179,313	4,674,000

14 American corporations
 5 European corporations
 1 Japanese corporation

Source: Fortune, May 1972; *Fortune*, August 1972.

The 20 Largest Industrial Corporations 1974

Rank	Company	Country	Sales ($000)	Net Income ($000)
1.	Exxon	US	42,061,336	3,142,192
2.	Royal Dutch/Shell	NE-GB	33,037,116	2,715,242
3.	General Motors	US	31,549,546	950,069
4.	Ford Motor	US	23,620,600	360,900
5.	Texaco	US	23,255,497	1,586,441
6.	Mobil Oil	US	18,929,033	1,047,446
7.	BP	GB	18,269,240	1,140,117
8.	Standard Oil California	US	17,191,186	970,018
9.	National Iranian Oil	Iran	16,802,000	N.A.
10.	Gulf Oil	US	16,458,000	1,065,000
11.	Unilever	GB-NE	13,666,667	362,807
12.	General Electric	US	13,413,100	608,100
13.	IBM	US	12,675,292	1,837,639
14.	ITT	US	11,154,401	451,070
15.	Chrysler	US	10,971,416	(52,094)
16.	Philips'	NE	9,422,386	273,493
17.	U.S. Steel	US	9,186,403	634,858
18.	Standard Oil (Ind.)	US	9,085,415	970,266
19.	Cie Française des Pétroles	FR	8,908,563	294,457
20.	Nippon Steel	Japan	8,843,550	113,099
	Total		348,500,747	18,575,308

13 American corporations
 5 European Corporations
 1 Japanese Corporation
 1 Iranian Corporation
Source: Fortune, August 1975

Appendix D

Energy Consumption per capita 1969

Rank	Country	SKE	Rank	Country	SKE
1	USA	10,773	29	Israel	2,314
2	Canada	8,819	30	Venezuela	2,096
3	Czechoslovakia	6,120	31	Panama	1,656
4	Sweden	5,768	32	Argentina	1,545
5	German Democratic		33	Spain	1,345
	Republic	5,673	34	Yugoslavia	1,293
6	Belgium & Luxembourg	5,429	35	Cyprus	1,252
7	Australia	5,214	36	Cuba	1,222
8	Denmark	5,141	37	Chile	1,210
9	United Kingdom	5,139	38	Greece	1,149
10	West Germany	4,850	39	Mexico	1,114
11	Trinidad and Tobago	4,727	40	Jamaica	1,088
12	Netherlands	4,659	41	Malta	994
13	Norway	4,430	42	Hong Kong	948
14	USSR	4,200	43	Uruguay	914
15	Poland	4,039	44	Guiana	896
16	Finland	3,575	45	Taiwan	884
17	France	3,517	46	Lebanon	764
18	Bulgaria	3,491	47	Singapore	761
19	Switzerland	3,175	48	Guam	750
20	Puerto Rico	3,075	49	Saudi Arabia	738
21	Austria	2,994	50	Gabon	659
22	Ireland	2,938	51	Korea Republic	634
23	Hungary	2,895	52	Peru	622
24	Japan	2,828	53	Iraq	614
25	South Africa	2,746	54	Albania	607
26	Rumania	2,627	55	Portugal	603
27	New Zealand	2,623	56	Colombia	578
28	Italy	2,432	57	Iran	565

(continued)

Rank	Country	SKE	Rank	Country	SKE
58	Lybia	559	94	Sri Lanka	133
59	South Rhodesia	541	95	El Salvador	118
60	Martinique	518	96	Indonesia	110
61	Syria	481	97	Sudan	108
62	Brazil	475	98	Guinea	95
63	Algeria	470	99	Sierra Leone	93
64	Turkey	461	100	Mauritania	93
65	Malaysia	450	101	Pakistan	90
66	British Honduras	449	102	Congo Democratic	
67	Fiji Islands	407		Republic	88
68	Liberia	390	103	Cameroon	84
69	Vietnam Republic	369	104	Tanzania	75
70	Costa Rica	332	105	Cambodia	65
71	Nicaragua	327	106	Togo	65
72	Jordan	308	107	Madagascar	64
73	Ecuador	269	108	Uganda	62
74	Philippines	266	109	Burma	54
75	Tunisia	248	110	Laos	54
76	Guatemala	236	111	Gambia	54
77	UAR (Egypt)	221	112	Zanzibar	44
78	Honduras	219	113	Malawi	40
79	Bolivia	213	114	Haïti	39
80	Dominican Republic	212	115	Central African Republic	38
81	Thailand	208	116	Dahomey	30
82	Republic of Congo	203	117	Ethiopia	29
83	Marocco	194	118	Nigeria	29
84	India	187	119	Somalia	28
85	Ivory Coast	183	120	Afghanistan	26
86	Moçambique	168	121	Chad	23
87	Mauritius	161	122	Nepal	17
88	Kenya	161	123	Mali	15
89	Equatorial Guinea	158	124	Yemen	14
90	Ghana	155	125	Niger	14
91	Angola	151	126	Upper Volta	11
92	Senegal	147	127	Rwanda	10
93	Paraguay	134	128	Burundi	8

Source: UN, *World Energy Supplies 1966–69*, ST/STAT/SER. J/14 (New York), 1972.

Defense Expenditures 1970
(in billions of US dollars at constant prices and exchange rates)

1	USA	59,319	25	Hungary[1]		513
2	USSR[1]	42,619	26	Indonesia		435
3	China	8,000[2]	27	Brazil		435
4	United Kingdom	4,604	28	South Korea		427
5	France	4,560	29	Pakistan		426
6	West Germany	4,112	30	Yugoslavia		401
7	Poland[1]	2,224	31	Saudi Arabia		387
8	East Germany[1]	1,990	32	Greece		385
9	Czechoslovakia[1]	1,741	33	Turkey		385
10	Italy	1,710	34	Taiwan		348
11	Canada	1,582	35	Switzerland		329
12	India	1,298	36	Argentina		320
13	Israel	1,268	37	Cuba		290
14	UAR (Egypt)	1,044	38	South Africa		285
15	Australia	927	39	Portugal		280
16	Japan	876	40	Bulgaria[1]		279
17	Rumania[1]	748	41	Norway		250
18	Sweden	747	42	Venezuela		248
19	The Netherlands	702	43	Denmark		225
20	Korea Republic	700[2]	44	Philippines		206
21	Iran	620	45	Iraq		202
22	South Vietnam	544	46	Thailand		195
23	North Vietnam	500[2]	47	Spain		181
24	Belgium	522	48	Mexico		168

(continued)

Source: *SIPRI Yearbook 1972*, (Stockholm 1972).

1. Current prices and exchange rates for the Warsaw Pact countries in accordance with Benoit-Lubell
2. estimated
3. Current prices and exchange rates for 1960
4. 1969

49	Syria	158	85	Guinea	14^2
50	Chile	157	86	Senegal	14
51	Colombia	136	87	Uganda	14^4
52	Cambodia	123	88	Yemen	14^2
53	Albania	119	89	Zambia	13^4
54	Austria	115	90	Afghanistan	12
55	Malaysia	115	91	Ivory Coast	12^4
56	Finland	113	92	Mali	12^2
57	Burma	112^3	93	Malagasy	11^4
58	Nigeria	110	94	Paraguay	11^2
59	Zaire	106	95	El Salvador	10^2
60	Singapore	100	96	Hong Kong	10^2
61	Algeria	99	97	Tanzania	10^4
62	Peru	95^2	98	Nicaragua	8^2
63	New Zealand	89	99	Cyprus	7
64	Jordan	76	100	Honduras	7
65	Kuwait	70	101	Luxembourg	7
66	Sudan	70	102	Somalia	7
67	Marocco	67	103	Congo Republic	6^4
68	Lybia	50	104	Costa Rica	6^2
69	Lebanon	45	105	Haïti	6
70	Ireland	38	106	Nepal	6^2
71	Dominican Republic	28	107	Mauritania	6
72	Ecuador	25^2	108	Burundi	5
73	Ethiopia	24	109	Central African Republic	5^2
74	Mongolia	23^3	110	Chad	5^4
75	Ghana	23^4	111	Dahomey	5^4
76	Laos	21	112	Upper Volta	4^4
77	Tunisia	21	113	Gabon	3^4
78	Rhodesia	20	114	Liberia	3^4
79	Uruguay	18^2	115	Malawi	3
80	Cameroon	16	116	Niger	3^4
81	Kenya	16	117	Togo	3
82	Guatemala	16	118	Sierra Leone	2
83	Bolivia	15^2	119	Panama	1^2
84	Sri Lanka	15^2			

International Liquidity, 1970
Gold holdings plus SDRs (special drawing rights) plus reserve position IMF plus foreign exchange, in millions of US $

1	USA	14,490	29	Republic of Korea	610
2	West Germany	13,610	30	Denmark	484
3	Italy	5,352	31	Finland	480
4	Switzerland	5,132	32	Iraq	462
5	France	4,960	33	Israel	449
6	Japan	4,840	34	Turkey	431
7	Canada	4,679	35	Algeria	389
8	The Netherlands	3,234	36	Chile	388
9	Belgium	2,847	37	Lebanon	386
10	United Kingdom	2,827	38	Peru	329
11	Spain	1,817	39	Greece	310
12	Austria	1,758	40	Panama	304
13	Australia	1,693	41	Singapore	294
14	Lybia	1,590	42	Jordan	256
15	Portugal	1,504	43	Philippines	251
16	Brazil	1,186	44	Nigeria	224
17	Venezuela	1,021	45	Kenya	220
18	South Africa	1,012	46	Iran	209
19	India	1,006	47	Cyprus	208
20	Thailand	906	48	Colombia	206
21	Norway	811	49	Kuwait	203
22	Sweden	761	50	Pakistan	182
23	Mexico	744	51	UAR (Egypt)	167
24	Malaysia	733	52	Jamaica	165
25	Ireland	696	53	Malta	158
26	Argentina	673	54	Marocco	141
27	Saudi Arabia	662	55	New Zealand	126
28	Taiwan	624	56	Ivory Coast	105

(continued)

Source: United Nations, Statistical Yearbook 1971 (New York, 1971), pp. 613–619.

57	Nepal	95
58	Burma	94
59	Ecuador	83
60	Cameroon	81
61	Guatemala	78
62	Ethiopia	71
63	Tanzania	65
64	El Salvador	63
65	Tunisia	60
66	Ghana	58
67	Uganda	57
68	Syria	54
69	Iceland	54
70	Nicaragua	49
71	Bolivia	46
72	Afghanistan	46
73	Trinidad and Tobago	43
74	Sri Lanka	42
75	Madagascar	37
76	Upper Volta	36
77	Sierra Leone	35

78	Togo	35
79	Dominican Republic	32
80	Malawi	29
81	Sudan	22
82	Senegal	22
83	Somalia	21
84	Guiana	20
85	Honduras	20
86	Niger	19
87	Paraguay	18
88	Costa Rica	17
89	Dahomey	16
90	Gabon	15
91	Republic of Congo	9
92	Ruanda	8
93	Haïti	4
94	Mauritania	3
95	Chad	2
96	Central African Republic	1
97	Mali	1

Some Basic Indicators of World Development 1950-1970

1. Population

	1969 in million	Percentage share of total world population	Average annual rate of growth 1963–69 in percent
Developed market economy countries	749	21	1.1
Developing countries	1,685	48	2.7
Socialist countries	1,127	31	1.6
World	3,561	100	2.0

Source: (1), p. 239.

2. Annual average growth rates of total and per capita gross domestic product at market prices by region, 1950–1970, in percent per year

	total			per capita		
	1950–60	1960–70	1969–70	1950–60	1960–70	1969–70
Developed market economy countries	4.1	4.9	2.7	2.8	3.7	1.6
Developing countries	4.7	5.2	6.3	2.4	2.5	3.5
Socialist countries	9.3	6.6	7.7	7.8	5.4	6.7

Source: (1), p. 247.

3. Gross National Product, per capita, 1969, in US $

Developed market economy countries   2590
Developing countries   200
Socialist countries   1190

Source: (1), p. 239.

4. World Trade, 1950–1970

— Annual Average Growth Rates of Exports in Percent

	1950–60	1960–70	1969–70
Developed market economy countries	7.0	10.0	15.6
Developing countries	2.9	7.2	11.3
Socialist countries	10.8	8.1	12.4
World	6.3	9.2	14.5

Source: (1), p. 22.

— World Exports by Origin and Destination 1950 and 1970 in Percent

	1950		1970	
From developed market economy countries		60.9		72.3
To developed market economy countries	41.0		55.8	
To developing countries	18.4		13.8	
To socialist countries	1.5		2.7	
From developing countries		31.0		17.3
To developed market economy countries	20.4		13.0	
To developing countries	8.4		3.4	
To socialist countries	2.2		0.9	
From socialist countries		8.1		10.4
To developed market economy countries	2.8		2.5	
To developing countries	1.2		1.4	
To socialist countries	4.1		6.5	
Total world exports in percentage		100.0		100.0
in billion US $		61.1		311.3

Source: (2), p. 78.

— Commodity Structure of Exports of Major Economic Classes, 1955, 1969, in Percentage

	Developed market economy countries (Class I)		Developing countries (Class II)		Socialist countries (Class III)	
	1955	1969	1955	1969	1955	1969
Food and beverages	15.5	11.2	32.5	23.8	16.5	13.8
Raw materials	14.4	8.9	29.4	19.6	21.4	12.1
Fuels	5.5	3.1	25.2	32.8	12.0	9.8
Machinery and transport equipment	24.8	35.4	0.5	2.2	23.1	31.5
other manufactures	39.8	41.4	12.4	21.6	27.0	32.8
Total above	100.0	100.0	100.0	100.0	100.0	100.0
of which primary commodities*	35.5	23.2	87.1	76.2	49.9	35.7
manufactured goods	64.5	76.9	12.9	23.8	50.1	64.3

*items 1–3
Source: (1), p. 193.

— Annual Average Growth Rate of Exports of Primary Commodities, 1955-1970, in Percentage

	1955-60	1960-67	1967-69
Developed market economy countries	4.8	5.6	6.7
Developing countries	2.5	4.4	9.2
Socialist countries	6.8	5.4	3.1

Source: (1), p. 193.

— Terms of Trade of Selected Trade Flows (1963 = 100)

	1953	1960	1965	1970
Developing areas/developed areas[1]	113	104	99	100
Other goods/manufactures[2]	116	102	98	91

1. Unit value index of exports from the first region to the second divided by unit value index of exports from the second to the first.
2. Unit value index of world exports of SITC sections 0–4 divided by unit value index of world exports of SITC sections 5–8.

Source: (1), p. 42.

5. Finance

— Total net Flow of Financial Resources from DAC Members to Less Developed
Countries and Multilateral Agencies, in Million US $

	Total official flows	Private flows	Total
1960	4,927	3,148	8,075
1965	6,290	4,170	10,460
1970	7,967	6,735	14,702

Source: (3), p. 173.

— Eighty Developing Countries, External Public Debt Outstanding, in Billion US$

1961	22
1965	37
1968	54
1970	67

Source: (2), p. 82.

— Average Terms of Loan Commitments of Official Bilateral Loans and Grants
to Less Developed Countries

	1964	*1968*	*1970*
Weighted average of the interest rates (in percentage)	3.1	3.3	2.8
Weighted average of the maturity of loans and grants (in years)	28.4	24.8	29.9

Source: 1964, 1968 — (4), Appendix II 32 1970 — (3), p. 63.

Sources:
(1) UN Handbook of International Trade and Development Statistics, 1972: UN
    TO / STAT. 4., New York 1973.
(2) World Bank, International Development Association, Annual Report, 1972
    Washington.
(3) OECD, Development Assistance, 1971 review. Paris 1972.
(4) Partners in Development — Report of the Commission on International
    Development (Pearson Report), Ottawa, 1969.

Countries with a Population Growth Rate of 3 and More Percent per Year

Dominican Republic	3.0
Ivory Coast	3.0
Liberia	3.0
Mongolia	3.0
Philippines	3.0
Ruanda	3.0
South Africa (inc. Namibia)	3.0
Tunisia	3.0
Algeria	3.1
Kenya	3.1
Malaysia	3.1
Peru	3.1
Thailand	3.1
Israel	3.2
Cambodia	3.2
Colombia	3.2
Costa Rica	3.3
Honduras	3.3
Panama	3.3
Rhodesia	3.3
Equador	3.4
Iraq	3.5
Jordan	3.5
Nicaragua	3.5
Venezuela	3.5
El Salvador	3.7

Source: World Bank Atlas 1972. International Bank for Reconstruction and Development, Washington, D.C., 1973.

Regional Distribution of Exports in Percent of World Total*

Regional Distribution of Exports in Percent of World Total*

| | Developed market economies | Developing countries | | | | Centrally planned economies |
		Total	Latin America	Africa	Asia	
1961–1965 (annual average)	66.75	21.03	5.48	4.46	9.53	11.52
1970	70.61	18.49	4.85	3.79	8.40	10.11
1971**	71.08	18.81	4.82	3.86	8.59	9.69

*The figures for the total world exports also include goods which are not comprised in the areas; therefore the sum of the shares is less than 100 percent.
**preliminary.
Source: International Development Association, Annual Report 1971, 1972.

Appendix J

International Efforts to Protect Man and the Biosphere

1. **1945.** Establishment of the United Nations Organization, UNESCO and FAO.
2. **1946.** Establishment of the World Health Organization.
3. **1948.** Establishment of the International Union for the Conservation of Nature and Natural Resources following an international conference sponsored by UNESCO and the government of France.
4. **1949.** United Nations Scientific Conference on the Conservation and Utilization of Resources, Lake Success, New York, August 17 to September 6.
5. **1955.** International Technical Conference on the Conservation of the Living Resources of the Sea, Rome, April 18 to May 16.
6. **1956.** Establishment of the International Atomic Energy Agency.
7. **1957-1958.** International Geophysical Year.
8. **1958.** Adoption of the Geneva Convention (treaty) on Fishing and Conservation of the Living Resources of the High Seas.
9. **1959.** Antarctic Treaty signed December 1 establishing the South Polar region as an international scientific reserve.
10. **1963.** Conference on Application of Science and Technology for the Benefit of Less Developed Areas, Geneva, February 4 to February 20.
11. **1964.** Inauguration of the International Biological Program.
12. **1966.** International Treaty on the Peaceful Use of Outer Space promulgated.
13. **1967.** Implementation of World Weather Watch under sponsorship of the World Meteorological Organization.
14. **1968.** UNESCO Intergovernmental Conference of Experts on the Scientific Basis for Rational Use and Conservation of the Resources of the Biosphere, Paris, September 4 to September 13.

15. **1968.** United Nations General Assembly Resolution 2398 (December 3) on the Problems of Human Environment.

16. **1970.** Establishment of the Scientific Committee on Problems of the Environment (SCOPE) by the International Council of Scientific Unions.

17. **1972.** United Nations Conference on the Human Environment, Stockholm, 1972.

Appendix K

Selected Scientific Institutes and Institutions which deal with International Political and Economic Problems

USA

Center for International Affairs
Harvard University
6 Divinity Avenue
Cambridge, Mass. 02138

World Order Models Project (WOMP)
11W 42nd Street
New York, N.Y. 10036

Northwestern University
Evanston, Ill.
(Simulation Methods)

University of Illinois
Research Center of Communications
Urbana, Ill.
(World Semantic Atlas)

World Data Project
Yale University
New Haven, Conn. 06520
(Aggregate Data)

Virginia Politechnical Institute
and State University
College of Arts and Sciences
Department of Political Science
Blacksburg, Va. 24061
(Aggregate Data World Handbook II)

University of Hawaii
Department of Political Science
Honolulu, Hawaii 96822

Interuniversity Consortium for
Political Research
Ann Arbor, Mich. 48106
(Voting and Survey Data)

Political Science Department
University of Michigan
Ann Arbor, Mich. 48106

Center for International Studies
MIT
Cambridge, Mass. 02139
(Simulation Methods)

CANADA

York University
Economic Research and Systems
Planning Group
Downsview 463/Toronto, Ont.

University of British Columbia
Department of Political Science
Vancouver, B.C.

UNITED KINGDOM

Peace and Conflict Research Program
University of Lancaster
Lancaster
(Simulation Methods and Models)

University of Sussex
Science Policy Research Unit
Nuffield Building Falmer
Brighton, Sussex

NETHERLANDS

Vrije Universiteit Amsterdam
De Boelelaan 1105
Amsterdam-Buitenveldert

USSR

Institute for Mathematics
USSR Academy of Science
Moscow

HUNGARY

Institute for Developing Countries
Hungarian Academy of Sciences
Budapest

FINLAND

Tampere Peace Research Institute
   (TAPRI)
Tampere

NORWAY

International Peace Research
   Institute Oslo (PRIO)
Oslo
(Galtung Structure Models and
   Gleditsch Distance Data)

European Consortium for Political
   Research
Data Information Service
Bergen
(Voting and Survey Data)

SWEDEN

Stockholm International Peace
   Research Institute (SIPRI)
Stockholm
(Armament Data)

BELGIUM

Union des Associations Inter-
   nationales (UAI)
Brussells
(ICO Data)

WEST GERMANY

Universität Mannheim
Mannheim

Battelle-Institut
Frankfurt a/M.

Hessische Stiftung Friedens- und
   Konfliktsforschung (HSFK)
Frankfurt a/M.
(Conflict Theory and Longseries
   Data [ZAPF])

ITALY

Club of Rome
Via Giorgione 163
Rome
(World Raw Materials and Environ-
   mental Protection)

FRANCE

Centre National des Recherches
   Scientifiques
Department de Sociologie
Paris

ARGENTINA

Fundación Bariloche
San Carlos de Bariloche and
Buenos Aires

Abbreviations

ASA	Association of Southeast Asia
ASEAN	Association of South-East Asian Nations
ASPAC	Asian and Pacific Council
BSP	Bruttosozialprodukt
CACM	Central American Common Market
CARIFTA	Caribbean Free Trade Association
DAC	Development Assistance Committee
ECAFE	Economic Commission for Asia and the Far East
ECCM	Eastern Caribbean Common Market
ECOSOC	Economic and Social Council
EFTA	European Free Trade Area
EWG	Europäische Wirtschaftsgemeinschaft
FAO	Food and Agriculture Organization
GATT	General Agreement on Tariffs and Trade
IBRD	International Bank for Reconstruction and Development
ICAO	International Civil Aviation Organization
IDA	International Development Agency
ILO	International Labour Organization
IMF	International Monetary Fund
ITU	International Telecommunication Union
IWP	Indicative World Plan
LAFTA	Latin American Free Trade Association
LINK-Projekt	Von nordamerikanischen, japanischen und europäischen Arbeitsgruppen konzipiertes ökonometrisches Weltmodell, das nationale Modelle untereinander verbinden soll. Projektkoordinator ist Prof. L. K. Klein, University of Pennsylvania.
NATO	North Atlantic Treaty Organization
OCAM	Organisation Commune Africaine et Malgache (Organization of African States and Madagascar)

OECD	Organization for Economic Cooperation and Development
RCD	Regional Co-operation for Development
SPC	South Pacific Commission
UDEAC	Central African Customs and Economic Union
UDEAO	West African Customs Union
UNCTAD	United Nations Conference on Trade and Development
UNDP	United Nations Development Programme
UNESCO	United Nations Scientific, Educational and Cultural Organization
UNICEF	United Nations Children's Fund
UNIDO	United Nations Industrial Development Organization
UNO	United Nations Organization
UPU	Universal Postal Union
WFP	World Food Programme
WHO	World Health Organization
WMO	World Meteorological Organization

● *North America, Western Europe, Oceania:*

1 USA	8 Austria	15 Finland
2 Canada	9 Denmark	16 Greece
3 Belgium-Luxemburg	10 Norway	17 Ireland
4 France	11 Portugal	18 Spain
5 Federated Republic of Germany	12 Sweden	19 Yugoslavia
	13 Switzerland	20 Australia
6 Italy	14 UK	21 New Zealand
7 Netherlands		

▲ *USSR and socialist countries in Eastern Europe:*

22 Bulgaria	24 German Democratic	26 Poland
23 Czechoslovia	Republic	27 Romania
	25 Hungary	28 USSR

○ *Latin America, nonsocialist countries in Asia and South Africa:*

29 Mexico	36 Panama	43 Israel
30 Trinidad, Tobago	37 Puerto Rico	44 Lebanon
31 Venezuela	38 Argentina	45 Hong Kong
32 Costa Rica	39 Chile	46 Japan
33 Guatemala	40 Peru	47 Malaysia
34 Jamaica	41 Uruguay	48 Libya
35 Nicaragua	42 Cyprus	49 South Africa

Source: GNP: World Bank Atlas 1972.
Energy Consumption: UN, World Energy Supplies, Statistical Papers, SER J, no. 6–15.

Bibliography

Adelman, E. and C.T. Morris. *Society Politics and Economic Development.* Baltimore: John Hopkins Press, 1967.

Attinger, E.O., ed., *Global Systems Dynamics.* Basel, München, New York, 1970.

Avramovic, D., et al. *Economic Growth and External Debt.* Baltimore 1964.

Baier, Kurt and Nicholas Rescher, *Values and the Future.* New York: The Free Press, 1971.

Balogh, Thomas. *The Economics of Poverty.* 1966.

Basler, E. *Strategie des Fortschritts.* Frauenfeld and Stuttgart 1972.

Beer, Stafford. *Brain of the Firm.* London 1972.

Benedict, Burton ed. *Problems of Smaller Territories.* London: Institute of Commonwealth Studies, University of London, 1967.

Binswanger, H. Chr. *Umweltschutz und Wirtschaftswachstum.* Frauenfeld: Verlag Huber, 1972.

Boettcher, E., Hgb. *Entwicklungstheorie und Entwicklungspolitik.* Tübingen, 1964.

Bouthoul, Gaston. *Kindermord aus Staatsräson.* Stuttgart: Deutsche Verlags-Anstalt, 1972.

BP Benzin und Petroleum Aktiengesellschaft. *Die Weltmineralölwirtschaft 1960–1970.* Hamburg, 1972.

BP Statistical Review of the World Oil Industry 1971 and 1972.

Choucri, N.; M. Laird; and D.H. Meadows. "Resource Scarcity and Foreign Policy: A Simulation Model of International Conflict." Paper presented at the Annual Meeting of the American Association for the Advancement of Science, January 1971, Philadelphia, Pennsylvania.

Codoni, R.; B. Fritsch; A. Melzer; J.F. Oertly; L. Sieber; and P. Walser. *World Trade Flows—Integrational Structure and Conditional Forecasts.* Vol. I and II. Zürich: Schulthess Polygraphischer Verlag AG, 1971.

Commoner, Barry. *The Closing Circle.* London: Jonathan Cape Ltd. 1972.

Cooper, R.N. *The Economics of Interdependence,* New York 1968.

Cosgrove, C.A. and K.J. Twitchett. *The International Actors: The UN and the EEC.* London, 1970.

Don, Arthur, et al. "A Blueprint for Survival." *The Ecologist* 2, 1 (January 1972).

Dror, Y. *Crazy States.* Lexington, Mass., Toronto, London, 1971.

Dunn, E.S., Jr. *Economic and Social Development.* Baltimore and London, 1971.

Ehrlich, P.R. *The Population Bomb.* New York: Ballantine, 1968.

ESSO AG Hamburg. "Gegenwärtige und künftige Probleme der Energieversorgung." Studie 7.

Feld, W.J. *Transnational Business Collaboration among Common Market Countries.* New York, Washington, London: Praeger Publishers, 1970.

Forrester, J.W. *World Dynamics.* Cambridge, Mass.: Wright-Allen Press, Inc., 1971.

—. *Urban Dynamics.* Cambridge, Mass.: The MIT Press, 1969.

—. "Counterintuitive Nature of Social Systems." *Technology Review*, no. 73, 1971.

Forward, Nigel. *The Field of Nations.* London: Macmillan Co., 1971.

Fritsch, B., Hgb. *Entwicklungsländer.* Kiepenheuer & Witsch, 1968.

—. "Wechselwirkung zwischen Gesellschaft und Technik." In *Systems 1969.* Stuttgart: Deutsche Verlags-Anstalt, 1970.

—. *Die Vierte Welt.* Stuttgart: Deutsche Verlags-Anstalt, 1970. Auflage dtv, München 1973.

Gabor, Dennis. *Der vernünftige Mensch.* Bern, Munchen, Wien. 1972.

Galtung, J. "From Value Dimensions for Social Analysis to Social Indicators." Manuscript, 1972.

Georgescu-Roegen, Nicholas. *The Entropy Law and the Economic Process.* Cambridge, Mass.: Harvard University Press, 1971.

Guth, W., Hgb. *Probleme der Wirtschaftspolitik in Entwicklungsländern.* Berlin 1967.

Hauser, J. *Die Grüne Revolution.* Zurich 1972.

Hesse, H. *Strukturwandlungen im Welthandel 1950–1960/61.* Tübingen 1967.

ILO (International Labour Office). "General Report: Recent Events and Developments in the Petroleum Industry." Petroleum Committee, Geneva 1973.

Institute of Development Studies. Sussex, Military Regimes. Bulletin, vol. 4, no. 4 (September 1972).

Johnson, H.G. *Economic Policies Toward Less Developed Countries.* Washington, D.C., 1967.

— *New Trade Strategy for the World Economy.* London 1969.

Joswig, H. and J.L. Schmidt, Hgb. *Aktuelle Probleme der Entwicklungsländer; Sammelband: Politische Okonomie, Neokolonialismus, Akkumulationsquellen, Außenwirtschaftsbeziehungen und wirtschaftliches Wachstum.* Berlin-Ost 1968.

Kende, István. *Local-Wars in Asia, Africa and Latin America, 1945–69.* Budapest: Center for Afro-Asian Research of the Hungarian Academy of Sciences, 1972.

Knorr, Klaus. *Power and Wealth: The Political Economy of International Power*. London: McMillan, 1973.

Lindbeck, Assar. *The Political Economy of the New Left*. New York, San Francisco, London, 1971.

Lloyd, P.J. *International Trade Problems of Small Nations*. Durham, N.C.: 1968.

Maddox, John. *Unsere Zukunft hat Zukunft*. Stuttgart: Deutsche Verlags-Anstalt, 1973.

McClelland, Ch.A. *Theory and the International System*. London: The Macmillan Co., 1966.

Maizels, Alfred. *Industrial Growth and World Trade*. Cambridge University Press, 1963.

Meadows, Dennis; Donella Meadows; Erick Zahn; and Peter Milling. *Grenzen des Wachstums*. Stuttgart: Deutsche Verlags-Anstalt, 1972.

Meadows, D.H. and J. Randers. "The Carrying Capacity of our Global Environment: A Look at the Ethical Alternatives." In *Western Man and Environmental Ethics*, edited by Ian Barbour. Reading, Mass.: Addison-Wesley, 1972.

Meadows, D.L. and D.H. Meadows, eds. *Toward Global Equilibrium: Collected Papers*. Cambridge, Mass. 1973.

Mesarovic, M.D.; D. Macko; and Y. Takahara. *Theory of Hierarchical. Multilevel Systems*. New York and London: Academic Press, 1970.

Naylor, Thomas H. *Computer Simulation Experiments with Models of Economic Systems*. New York, London, Sydney, Toronto, 1971.

"The no-Growth Society." Daedalus, *Journal of the American Academy of Arts and Sciences*. Fall 1973.

Odum, H.D. *Environment, Power and Society*. New York, London, Sydney, Toronto, 1971.

Peccei, A. *The Chasm Ahead*. London: The McMillan Co., 1969.

__. "The Predicament of Mankind." *Successo* XII, 6, New Series (June 1970).

Pearson, Lester B., chairman. *Partners in Development*. Report of the Commission on International Development. New York 1969.

Pincus, J.A., ed. *Reshaping the World Economy, Rich and Poor Countries*. Englewood Cliffs, N.J.: Prentice-Hall, 1968.

__ *Economic Aid and International Cost Sharing*. The Rand Corp. 1965.

Prebisch, Ráoul. *Towards a New Trade Policy for Development*. New York: United Nations, 1964.

__. *Change and Development, Latin Americas Great Task*. Washington, D.C.: Inter-American Development Bank, 1970.

Rapaport, Jacques; Ernest Muteba; and Joseph J. Therattil. *Small States and Territories, Status and Problems*. New York: UNITAR, 1971.

Remington, R.A. *The Warsaw Pact*. Cambridge, Mass.: MIT Press, 1971.

Robinson, E.A.G., ed. *Economic Consequences of the Size of Nations*. London, 1960.

Rubin, S.J. *The Conscience of the Rich Nations: The Development Assistance Committee and the Common Aid Effort*. New York and London, 1966.

Ruge, F. *Bündnisse unter besonderer Berücksichtigung von UNO, NATO, EWG und Warschauer Pakt in Vergangenheit und Gegenwart*. Frankfurt, 1971.

Russett, B.M. *International Regions and the International System: A Study in Political Ecology.* Rand McNally, 1969.

Senghaas, D., Hgb. *Kritische Friedensforschung.* Frankfurt 1971.

—, Hgb. *Imperialismus und strukturelle Gewalt; Analysen über abhängige Reproduktionen.* Frankfurt 1972.

—. *Rüstung und Militarismus.* Frankfurt 1972.

Smith, S.A. de. *Microstates and Micronesia.* New York, London, 1970.

Stahel, A.A. *Die Anwendung der numerischen Mathematik und der Simulationstechnik bei der Darstellung des Ablaufs einer internationalen Krise.* Frauenfeld, 1973.

Stapledon, Olaf. *Last and First Man and Last Man in London.* Penguin Books Ltd., 1972.

The Statement's Year-Book 1972/73 und 1973/74. London, 1972, 1973.

Steinbuch, K., et al. *Die humane Gesellschaft.* Stuttgart, 1972.

—. *Kurskorrektur.* Stuttgart, 1973.

Stöber, G.J. and D. Schumacher. *Technology Assessment and Quality of Life.* Amsterdam, London, New York, 1973.

Stockholm International Peace Research Institute (SIPRI). *The Arms Trade with the Third World.* Stockholm, New York, 1971.

Taylor, Ch.L and N.C. Hudson. *World Handbook of Political and Social Indicators.* 2nd ed. New Haven and London, 1972.

Taylor, G.R. *Das Selbstmordprogramm.* Fischer-Taschenbuch nr. 1369. Frankfurt 1973.

UNCTAD. *Towards a Global Strategy of Development.* Report by the Secretary-General of the United Nations Conference on Trade and Development to the Second Session of the Conference. New York: United Nations, 1968.

United Nations. *Planning and Plan Implementation.* New York, 1967.

—. *Development and Environment.* Founex Report. New York, 1971.

—. *World Plan of Action for the Application of Science and Technology to Development.* New York, 1971.

—. *World Energy Supplies 1961–1970.* Statistical Papers, series J, no. 15. New York, 1972.

Vickers, Geoffrey. *Freedom in a Rocking Boat.* Middlesex: Pelican Book, 1972.

Vital, David. *The Inequality of States.* Oxford: Clarendon Press, 1967.

Waterston, Albert. *Development Planning, Lessons of Experience.* Baltimore, 1965.

Wellmann, B., Hgb. *Die Umweltrevolte.* Köln 1972.

Wiener, Norbert. *God & Golem, Inc.* Cambridge, Mass.: MIT Press, 1964.

—. *Decision and Control.* London, New York, Sydney, Toronto, 1966.

—. *Cybernetics and Management.* 2nd ed. Reprint. London, 1971.

Williams, B.R., ed. *Science and Technology in Economic Growth.* London: The International Economic Association, 1973.

Willrich Mason. *Civil Nuclear Power and International Security.* New York, Washington, London: Praeger Publishers, 1971.

World Bank. "Urbanisation." Sector Working Paper. 1972.
—. *Environmental, Health and Human Ecologic Considerations in Economic Development Projects.* Washington, D.C., 1973.
Yearbook of International Organisations. 13th ed. (1970–71). Brüssel 1971.

About the Author

Bruno Fritsch is presently professor of Economics at the Swiss Federal Institute of Technology (Eidgenössische Technische Hochschule Zürich—ETHZ), Zurich, Switzerland, where he heads the Division for Basic Research. In addition, he is co-director of both the Center for Economic Research and the Interdisciplinary Postgraduate Course on Problems of the Developing Countries of the ETHZ. Fritsch holds degrees from the University of Prague and the University of Basel, and has taught at Harvard, the College d'Europe, Bruges, Belgium, the University of Basel, and the Australian National University Research School for Pacific Studies, Canberra.

Mr. Fritsch has represented the German and Swiss governments on numerous international commissions and studies and has participated in many ECAFE and International Future Research conferences. He has published extensively in both Switzerland and Germany. His English language publications include the present volume and *World Trade Flows—Integrational Structure and Conditional Forecasts* (Center for Economic Research, 1971).